WINNING THE WAR AGAINST CONCUSSIONS IN YOUTH SPORTS

Brain & Life Saving Solutions for Preventing & Healing Middle-High School & College Sports Head Injuries

William White MSN
Alan Ashare MD
Katharine White MSN

William T. White, MSN/ Publisher: Create Space
33 College Hill Rd. Suite 29A
Warwick, RI 02886
www.BrainInPlay.com

Printed in the United States of America
First Printing 2014

Disclaimer:

Publisher: Create Space Publishing
Book Design: Ashley Barge & William White

Winning The War Against Concussions In Youth Sports
William T. White, MSN -- 1st Ed.
ISBN 13: 978-1500547592

DEDICATION & ACKNOWLEDGEMENTS

This Book is dedicated to all youth sports players and their families who have experienced a significant sports-related head injury.

*"It's not the years in your life that count.
It's the life in your years."
~Abraham Lincoln*

This acknowledgment page will never be able to express the enormous gratitude we have toward all family, friends and colleagues that have helped us along on the journey to complete this book.

Specifically, on the process of writing this book we acknowledge:
- All youth athletes/families who shared their stories
- Mentors Dr. Ed Iannuccilli and Dr. Bob Coli
- Ashley Barge, Executive Assistant/Marketing Consultant
- Donna & Bob, Matt Fraser, Brian & Bobbi, Gina, Matt & Izzy
- Advisors Amber Clarke, Wayne Stone, Michael Monti, Tom Smith, Jami & Michael Uretsky & Madeline, Dan Guglielmo and Father Nic
- NFL Vets Spencer Larsen, Tommy Clayton & Patrick Pass
- Our Block Island Summer Community, especially Bo Gempp, LisaS., Steve Filippi & Ballard's Staff, Danielle, O/Port Launch Drivers, and Musicians World Premier Band, Shawn David Allen & John Brazile
- BankRI Family & Coach Digit Murphy-World Champ Boston Blades
- Our Healthtrax Family, Joan Pelly, Chad Bianchi and Barbara Cunha
- Dr. Ann McKee, Officer Joe Shig., MFH, Dr.K., BriggsD. & BettyG.

Simply put we will never forget the way all of you made us feel as you supported us to be our best selves during a time of challenge.

CONTENTS

CHAPTER ONE

PRELUDE

"The world we have made as a result of the level of thinking we have done thus far creates problems we cannot solve at the same level of thinking at which we created them."

~ Albert Einstein

Not all youth sports head injuries are preventable. But our mission at Brain In Play International is to prevent as many as possible, facilitate healing those that do occur, and help athletes avoid long-term brain injury consequences. We intend to make this happen by **empowering players, parents, and coaches (*dubbed going forward as "the Big-3"*)** by providing them with the core knowledge, brain wellness best practices, activation tools, culture model, and confidence necessary to leverage top brain wellness and brain functioning.

Given all that is happening with youth sports head injuries, this is really a book about hope—hope for the safest and most satisfying future for young athletes and their brains as they play competitive sports from middle/high-school through college. Hope, that armed with the knowledge and a fresh perspective gained from the latest neuroscience research, a break-through solution based on two new biosciences, and a unique youth sports honor culture, the Big-3 will quickly advance their way of thinking and behaving about brain health in relation to youth sports. **Hope, that with Brain In Play's novel paradigm, the alarm that has been sounded about youth concussions by the Center for Disease Control and The Institute of Medicine will be silenced and the brains and lives of youth playing contact sports will be safer, enriched, and protected from catastrophic brain damage.** In the final analysis, a combined brain wellness and sports culture prototype is the only way thought leaders can simultaneously safeguard and stimulate the brain development of young athletes in the United States and around the globe. This of course will help save the sports that most youth love to play, greatly benefit from, and many live for—and that parents and coaches love to watch and supervise.

This means getting as many of the Big-3 to know about, practice, and support brain-healthy best practices which help prevent and heal concussive, subconcussive, and catastrophic brain injuries and their consequences, while avoiding brain-unhealthy habits which not only increase the risk of sports head injuries, but delay healing. Indeed, effectively spreading the word about the power of brain wellness by involving those who care the most sets the stage for changing the world, one big threesome, league, school or community at a time.

The Big-3 needs to know some things right up front about what this book represents—starting with there will likely be some traditionalists in medicine and sports that will not appreciate that it significantly empowers the Big-3, especially players and parents. The biggest reason there has not been more progress to date on the issue of sports head injury is a failure to collaborate—which has to do with many powerful forces that have not lined up to make this happen (and to not be naïve, yet others that have lined up in support of biases unfavorable to changing the status quo). However *there is too much on the line with youth sports and too much that we have learned to not push the envelope.* Thus, educate and empower the Big-3 we will, because this book is ultimately about providing leadership, and true leaders do the right things regardless of what the potential responses might be from those with different agendas and incentives.

The two groups that have been most left out of the 'communication-collaboration mix' by too many, are youth athletes and parents. The justification for this may have at first been well-meaning (i.e., "We don't want to scare young people or their parents," or "Let's not cause a major crisis until we learn more"), but given what we now know, it's a bit 'old school' in this day and age to not educate more openly and invite collaboration with players and parents. By not doing we set these groups up to be left with unreliable alternatives such as the Internet and TV. Very few parents have access to comprehensive sports brain injury and wellness updates and student-athletes generally must rely on coaches for detailed sports brain injury information, most who feel ill-prepared and are requesting more coach training themselves to better understand this sports head injury challenge.

In the words of two-time U.S. Olympic women's soccer team gold medalist goalie Brianna Scurry during a conversation we had in May of 2014, "With the current state of affairs, it took a high profile athlete in her thirties as well-connected as me four years to really understand my concussion and get some of the right help I needed—and I'm still recovering. I can only imagine how I would have handled this as a younger athlete!" I'll reserve further comment for now about how anything short of *"full disclosure with careful translation and practical takeaways"* is a slippery slope that limits the Big-3 from making the best decisions regarding sports head injuries based on informed consent—except to applaud those early advocates who worked hard to improve awareness, education and culture. These pioneers are led by Sports Legacy Institute's Chris Nowinski, Dr. Bob Cantu and Dr. Ann McKee, Mom's Team, Professor Douglas Abrams and our very own Dr. Alan Ashare (second author and Brain In Play International's Sports Head Injury Concussion Safety Adviser), to name a select few.

This book is written primarily on behalf of middle/high school and college-age athletes, because you are the ones whose brains are at greatest risk from head injuries given the ***perfect storm combination***:

(1) The brains of players under age twenty-one through twenty-four are still maturing – thus these brains are more vulnerable to injury;

(2) Youth sports have a higher incidence of brain injury (multiple millions play middle/high school and college contact sports daily worldwide);

(3) The unique way some younger brains/bodies are biomechanically affected by sports impacts;

(4) The reality of extreme "resource variation" involving head injury awareness, assessment, and treatment alternatives across the universe of youth sports in communities across the globe; and

(5) The powerful influence the youth sports culture exerts over players to not speak up when hurt and "gut" things out, to please coaches, older players and parents, and avoid the likely potential of losing playing time.

All of this is critically important, because youth head injuries are very complicated and selectively involve the brain in ways that very often go underappreciated or unnoticed by well-meaning and caring clinicians. This can cause and/or worsen the biopsychosocial consequences of sports brain damage, which can in turn harm a range of neurologic operations from executive brain functions (judgment and decision-making) to mood stabilization and cognitive-academic performance. Of most concern is that these injuries are unpredictably tricky, as the same athlete can suffer three "big impact" concussions with seemingly uncomplicated recoveries only to have a fourth "minor impact" glancing blow to the side of the head result in a persistent post-concussive syndrome lasting several months or even years.

As you will learn, the authors have a high degree of faith that it will be youth athletes, and their parents and coaches, that will help save the day when it comes to spreading the word about how sports head injuries can be reduced, prevented, and better healed by optimizing brain health (optimized meaning the best brain wellness and functioning possible—to offset brain damage vulnerabilities before, during, and after head trauma in a number of achievable ways).

To complete this prelude, three other priorities require mention. First, as part of designing a fast-track brain injury prevention, healing and consequence-avoidance system for youth, we included a culture change innovation to quickly adjust the philosophy that now perpetuates youth sports around playing head hurt that can be readily adopted. With combined more than ten decades of coaching, team physician

Author Bill White (left) talks brain health on NFL Vet Tom Clayton's PBS Show

and clinician scientist experience, this book's three authors know that brain/behavioral science is one thing, and the practical realities involving the management of teams, games and practice situations are quite another—so culture transformation involving an aligned code of honor and conduct that "works" for youth sports will be necessary to powerfully activate, sustain, and spread significant change.

Second, **the biggest emerging issue in youth sports head injury isn't concussions**, but what are called **subconcussive blows that accumulate** (abbreviated as **A-SCBs**). Thanks to new advanced imaging/analysis MRIs (magnetic resonance imaging) called **DTI (Diffuse Tensor Imaging) Scans**, we now know A-SCBs alone cause similar brain damage changes as concussions do over the course of only one season of high school or college sports.[1,2] When A-SCBs combine with concussions, advanced imaging shows even greater damage to both the brain's makeup (structure) and how it functions[3] (just confirmed in a breakthrough study as we go to press), which some researchers propose increases potential for long-term consequences.[4]

What are A-SCBs? Most readers are familiar with the term concussion, defined at the last meeting of world experts (Zurich December, 2012) as a brain injury that is a complex pathophysiological process caused by biomechanical forces resulting in acute clinical symptoms that disrupt how the brain is functioning.[5] The basic translation: The brain as a whole and its' fragile cells (made up of margarine-like consistency) gets hurt upon crashing against the hard skull due to forces that cause the brain to accelerate and stop quickly (think of an egg yolk inside a hard shell). When this start-stop biomechanical force is powerful enough, a concussion happens (causing a release in the brain of a neurometabolic cascade of biochemicals harmful to brain cells).[6] At the same time, some of the brain's communication cells called axons are stretched too far too fast by this dynamic force and break. This dual trauma explains many of concussion's symptoms, as some brain cells are toxically damaged and die, and others responsible to send complex messages throughout the brain are basically cut in half.[6]

A-SCBs are best thought of as many, many less powerful mini-start and stops, which over time exert a major damaging effect on brain cells. Think of taking an apple and throwing it against a wall (concussion) versus tapping it on the wall a hundred times (A-SCBs). Given the way the brain's fragile cells respond to a big crash against the skull or hundreds of mini-traumas, it's understandable why we need to prevent and offset both of these conditions—particularly for youth brains that we have learned are more ravaged by such injuries.

Lastly, while written for the Big-3 and primarily players, this book is *dedicated to those youth sports players and their families who are suffering through major sports-related head injuries*. Authors Dr. Alan Ashare, my clinician scientist wife Katharine, and I have had the great privilege of getting to know many of you—some after the passing of your loved ones—and we know that with catastrophic or chronically symptomatic head injuries it never really ends. We can't begin to tell you how much you have touched and enriched our lives and given us renewed courage, energy, inspiration and purpose to address and change for the better how youth contact sports and healthcare manages head injuries. And in keeping with our Brain In Play International philosophy, which is aligned with yours as some of you have told us, we want to share with you our ultimate intention:

No head-injured youth athlete should ever be left in danger or behind.

Nathan Stiles - High-School Football/Basketball Player, Kansas
The Light Behind The Nathan Project: www.NathanProject.com
Sports Head Injured October 28, 2010: Second Impact Syndrome

CHAPTER TWO

A Preface for All Brain Performance Enhancement^{sm} (BPE)

"Our lives begin to end the day we become silent about things that matter."

~ *Martin Luther King Jr.*

Brain In Play International has designed a new brain wellness system for contact sports players from youth athletics to the pros based on Nobel Prize research principles and two leading-edge medical biosciences. It helps prevent, heal, and possibly avoid the long-term consequences of sports head injuries by putting a **helmet of protection and performance enhancement where it belongs—all over the brain on every cell possible**. The system combines specific brain health best practices with behavioral success-activators to improve the functioning, preservation and growth of brain cells.

This patent-pending system is called **Brain Performance Enhancement^{sm} (BPE)**. This book unveils a customized youth version of this all-natural brain wellness system called **BPE Youth Fast-Track** for middle/high school through college student athletes, parents and coaches (and "difference-makers" behind the scenes: athletic directors, sports officials and teachers). **The reason is that because of**

youth sports head injuries, youth brain health is at stake world-wide, a reality that has even captured the attention of world leaders and top U.S. medical policy advisors (i.e., **President Obama's White House Concussion Summit**, May 29, 2014 and The Institute of Medicine's Youth Concussion Committee's October 2013 report). *When a medical issue attracts this much focus it means that someone knows an emerging public health crisis looms large.*

We have been advised by youth sports players, thought-leading physician concussion experts, national parent advocates, top youth/pro coaches, and professional athletes that BPE Youth Fast-Track, which also includes an inventive youth sports culture-change process, will strongly contribute to saving youth contact sports. We consider this important but highly secondary to helping prevent damage to, and improving the wellness of, the most important body part of all youth participating in sports, academics, and life in general—their brains.

While we acknowledge that great strides have been made in the last few years **making sports safer for youth players** with improvements to equipment, rules, concussion awareness/education, and sideline assessment and care, much more still needs to be done as soon as possible. Why, you ask? Multiple recent surveys presented at the 2013–2014 annual meetings of key physician specialty groups tell us **the majority of youth will still play "head-hurt" and hide concussion symptoms from parents and coaches.**[8, 9] Suffering any additional head injury while playing hurt greatly increases the potential for serious short- and long-term brain damage, ranging from being academically and athletically problematic in the least, to being fatally catastrophic or developing long-term brain damage and diseases including various dementias such as CTE, as readers will discover.

Brain In Play's approach is truly game changing. It is unique, yet complementary to traditional sports safety strategies—as we specifically focus on **making players and their brains safer for sports** (versus making sports safer for players). It is also about quickly getting to the heart of who and what really matters most when dealing with youth sports head injuries.

Who and what matters the most are players and their brain health, followed closely by parents and youth coaches. As coined in the prelude, we will call this high-profile threesome **the Big-3**. This is because the best and quickest way to turn around youth sports head injuries, such that most injuries will be prevented or managed with newly emerging brain wellness best practices, will only be possible if the Big-3 works closely together as a team. This can happen in small units (individual player/team situations) or on larger scales (youth leagues, schools, conferences, and larger national organizations).

Another essential matter is to create the greatest sense of urgency possible about youth sports head injuries for the Big-3 and other interested stakeholders. Why? This necessity is driven by late-breaking sports head injury research developments that many Big-3 may not be aware of, such as: *early stage chronic traumatic encephalopathy (CTE) dementia has been discovered in seventeen- and eighteen-year-old athletes*, as well as a soccer player in his twenties.[11] Further, new tech brain imaging on concussed youth (DTI scans) surprisingly showed *significant brain damage still present four months following a concussion, after most youth players are free of recognizable symptoms*, have passed their standard sports neuropsych tests, and have long-since returned to their classrooms and sports.[12]

These types of worrisome discoveries are validated as we go to press with yet another groundbreaking study from July 2014 revealing *college football players with no history of concussion had DTI scans showing marked shrinkage of a key brain part that manages memory and learning compared to a group of college peers, suggesting this outcome is from accumulated subconcussive blows*. **A third group of players in the study with concussion histories had even greater brain shrinkage**.[3] While no one can definitively draw conclusions from this study with 100% certainty, if one factors in previously published research on concussions and A-SCBs in youth populations (that you will learn more about in this book), it is prudent to say this is very concerning news and merits our close attention.

Additional new research findings that all Big-3 should immediately know about are presented in Chapter 7 along with key practical take-aways for players, parents, and coaches. While this book is not an academic research effort, it is informed by detailed scientific information and references should players, parents, or coaches want more follow-ups about anything they may read.

However, this book will not seek to recreate the wheel and repeat what other clinician-scientist authors in their particular fields of expertise have already documented extensively. Therefore, we will not address medical sideline management, diagnosis, emergency care, or return to play in any detail. We will, however, identify some excellent references throughout this book should readers desire to pursue best practice knowledge regarding any of these issues. And just in time the American Academy of Neurology[13] has stepped up to provide excellent one to three page primers on these and other sports head injury matters (PDF links available at AAN's site www.AAN.com and Brain In Play International's website www.BrainInPlay.com).

Before closing, I want to emphasize Brain In Play International and all three book authors are *major supporters* of youth sports, given the substantial biopsychosocial advantages sports offers to youth athletes. We suspect **the Big-3 also shares our excitement about jump-starting brain wellness that also enhances athletic performance, improves academics, and boosts general wellbeing**. So then, this book is not just about brain injury prevention and healing, but is also about improving '*academic, athletic, health, and life*' performance.

We want to underscore up front that for players with concussion histories, prevention-maintenance based on a best practice brain enhancement model is a best hedge to avoid additional concussions and minimize concerns about long-term consequences—every player, parent, and coach's worst fear these days. While the BPE-Youth Fast Track itself is not a therapeutic head injury initiative (like Brain In

Play International's original **Brain Performance Enhancement**sm System), for healthy youth athletes it is a great self-management add-on that helps improve brain wellness and functioning, such that future risks for head injury are reduced (further explained in Chapters 9-11).

B. White proposes this book at BIP's Annual Meeting: New England Patriot's Patriot Place Renaissance Hotel Presidential Board Room in December 2013

And finally in what likely is an all-time first for a book of this type, *we will not just be proposing* a brain saving wellness system that includes a culture change activator to address youth sports concussive head injuries. We will also be asking the Big-3 to help carry forward the message this book offers to both stop young players from playing head-hurt and to improve their brain resilience to prevent and/or help offset concussive and subconcussive injuries (led primarily by youth athletes). Specifically we are asking middle/high school and college athletes to spread the word ASAP about this brain and life-saving BPE Youth Fast-Track system and Honor Code through Tweeting, Face-booking and You-Tubing to friends, families and colleagues across their neighborhoods, schools, states, the nation and globe.

To make this fun and spirited we suggest a ***dance-off challenge*** for those so inclined, as well as providing other social-media communication blueprints (see Chapter 18). And in recognition of *crowd* *sourcing*, we welcome suggestions on how we can improve on BPE Youth's Best Practices and Honor Code to be even better.

What Winston Churchill[14] said more than a few generations ago in relation to another type of war very much applies to how this book can help us all to do our part to defeat or at least marginalize youth sports head injuries and their consequences:

> *Now this [book] is not the end. It is not even the beginning of the end—but it is, perhaps, the end of the beginning.*
>
> *~ Winston Churchill*

The point of this adapted quote, beyond confirming youth sports head injuries are a faster growing more serious problem than most stakeholders previously realized, is to rally the Big-3 "troops". There is no time to waste. Indeed, it is time to empower the Big-3 to take action based on what is already known and being corroborated almost daily by the latest neuroscience research findings. Head injuries have already victimized too many of our loved ones. To close on this preface for all it is Brain In Play International's intention to pronounce:

The beginning of youth sports head injury awareness and education is over. It is time now to add to the awareness/education done to date AND take extreme action based on what we know today in support of those who play, lovingly watch and coach youth games, to improve the brain health of all youth sports players and prevent all head-hurt athletes from ever playing while still injured.

CHAPTER THREE

For Players Only

"To complement what the NFL is doing to make sports safer for its players, why don't we make players and their brains safer for sports!" ~ Author, Katharine White 2013

This is probably another first: A preface for players that informs busy, scheduled-challenged youth it's OK to skip some chapters in this book (for now) and provides a *fast-read* version. Why, you ask? Time, focus, and importance! When I was playing sports in high school and later when I was going to college, sports was my life close to 24-7. I did manage to fit in some fun, along with a part-time job, a relationship and the required schoolwork, but I knew what my priorities were: playing football, soccer, baseball, and basketball—eventually winding down to hard-core street hockey and basketball. And today, time is even harder to come by for most student athletes, whether playing organized sports or not. As you will find out, this book is about more than reading and learning facts—it's about empowering you to enhance your brain wellness and athletic performance, so sports can be as safe, rewarding, and fun as it gets.

As a student the only way I would have considered reading a book I didn't have to was if I heard that someone actually understood, and went out of his or her way to make the book reasonably short and to the point, and told me what important parts to read and the parts I could skip. Also, if I heard that it pulled together some things that were very important to me—like sports and my brain, or the brains of my teammates, and asked me to give some feedback when convenient to help make the book's content even better, now that would have sparked my interest. Finally, I might have actually read it word for word if I was asked to participate in a call to action to change the youth sports world that improved my chances big-time for:

➢ A better sports experience—starting now and going forward;
➢ Avoiding a major head injury resulting in lost playing time;
➢ Avoiding the possibility of lingering brain damage;
➢ All natural enhanced athletic performance—by tweaking just a few key things;
➢ Improved academic performance (with same tweaks above);
➢ Improved life performance (better: relationships, mood, focus, and general health and wellness);
➢ Helping teammates and younger players to avoid head injuries;
➢ Helping save youth contact sports—now being threatened by sports head injuries.

[1] Most middle school girl soccer players report playing with concussion symptoms, and then go unchecked by a qualified medical provider[11]

Thus, I have written this player preface—where on the last page of this chapter I indicate which chapters are must-reads for the student athlete who is schedule-challenged. This *fast-read* supports as many youth as possible to get up to speed on the latest head injury facts, learn about subconcussions, and to discover a new injury prevention and performance solution that all youth should know about.

So what exactly is this book about, how do players fit in, why is it so important, and who is writing it?

This book is about a brain wellness solution designed for youth athletes called **Brain Performance Enhancement Youth Fast-Track** or **BPE Youth** that will help fix the biggest challenge facing middle/high school and college sports today: sports head injuries (notice I didn't say concussions, because as you will find out, scientists are learning concussions might not be the most concerning head injury the majority of youth players face). It is also about involving and educating the most important group that has been left out of the youth sports head injury problem: *you,* **the players**. That's where you come in. This book prioritizes you by giving you detailed information in understandable terms about brain health and wellness based on the latest research and newest science. **The buy-in for players**: enhanced athletic, *academic* and life performance, injury prevention, and, if you get concussed, access to a best-practice healing and consequence avoidance solution *that, in large part, you can self-manage once your recovery progresses and your doctor signs off on it.*

Much of this challenges traditional old-school medical thinking that says we should protect youth (and parents) from the scary details about sports head injuries. Of course this approach didn't work for previous generations in the public health wars on drugs and teenage pregnancy—and that was before we-all had the Internet, smartphones, and mobile devices which most twelve-year-olds know how to use to access the same medical information as providers (as well spurious healthcare advice that can't be trusted).

We need middle/high school and college players to weigh in about sports head injuries and get actively involved in turning things around (to give the adults who are running the show your feedback so that, going forward, youth can help run the show). The bottom line here is that the more you know about the basics of sports brain injuries, the more you can help inform needed improvements and spread the word to peers and younger players. They will listen to and hear you better, before listening to many adults.

We also want you to participate with willing parents and coaches to embrace or adapt our code of youth sports honor and conduct around head injuries, so that no head-injured player will ever be put in a position where they are left in danger or behind and could get badly hurt. If this sounds like a U.S. Military Special Forces mantra, well it is similar. Make no mistake about it: we are fighting a war against sports-related brain injuries, and should we not start winning decisively, more young brains and lives will be unnecessarily damaged—and the future of youth contact sports will be at risk.

Two of this book's authors are a clinician scientist couple with advanced clinical degrees in brain/behavioral health who parented five high school athletes and thoroughly enjoyed it—except when sports injuries struck, in particular a series of concussive head injuries with their fourth child. The dad (me) for two decades coached three of the top highest-risk concussion youth sports while also being the second-in-command at the nation's first brain/behavioral health hospital for youth under 21. The company my wife and I own today sponsors the 2013 world champion professional *women's ice-hockey* team (Boston Blades), the sport along with women's soccer that shares the highest *player per hours practiced/played* concussion rate. So we have a very personal stake in turning this youth sports head injury issue around. It is my voice that you will hear most throughout this book.

My coauthor wife Katharine White was a Division I college athlete starting as a freshman, never missed one of our children's games, and co-developed Brain In Play's Brain Performance Enhancement solution as a clinician scientist and organizational development specialist with more than two decades of experience as a psychotherapist.

Book coauthor, Dr. Alan Ashare, has been an international youth sports head injury physician safety advocate for more than 25 years and **originated the "Heads Up – Don't Duck" program** directing USA Hockey's Safety Committee back in the mid-1990s, now adapted by all major sports. His many youth sports volunteer positions include leading multiple state interscholastic high-school medical committees, national hockey safety/equipment councils, and the global organization setting standards for sports equipment safety. Dr. Ashare has served as team physician for multiple USA Hockey Junior World Championship Teams. He played college football at Columbia, was an officer in the U.S. Air Force and raised four high school athletes. Known affectionately as 'Doc' by the raft of professional and amateur hockey players and coaches he has advised through the years, he just released the leading book on the biomechanics of sports concussions in May 2014. **Doc has been there and done that in so many sports safety roles that his knowledge and experience regarding the universe of youth sports head injury safety may be unparalleled.**

To repeat, all three authors are big supporters of youth sports, primarily because of the many advantages sports affords young people, not the least of which includes developing team-player, problem-solving, leadership, and self-esteem competencies. But truth be known, we are also youth sports fans because, for the most part, the beauty and pureness of competition has not been tarnished.

In closing our player preface, we hope to strongly connect with you as a group of players. We may be adult clinician scientists, but we are also big fans of the youth of today that play sports. We are very aware of the sacrifices youth sports players must make *today* to be the best they can be for their teams, coaches, and loved ones, and we sincerely appreciate your attention and consideration around this call to action book, wherever in the world you may live and play. Help us to help you make youth sports the best it can be by learning how to safely and proactively prevent sports head injuries so as many as possible don't happen in the first place —now and for the next generation. On the next page is the book's **student athlete fast-read version** as promised, **highlighted in gray**...but see what's in next paragraph.

Chapter 18 shows how athletes can best spread the word about this book's call to action. We suggest a dance-off challenge using your favorite social media (You-Tube, Instagram etc.) that you post on our Facebook page, which we hope middle/high school and college athletes participate in and get others to compete on! If adults can do it for an important cause like ALS, youth can make it happen too for sports head injury's BPE Youth brain/life-saving solutions. If the results are great for any individual, team or organization we will promptly report this out through our national press connections and on Brain In Play's Facebook page. Now you can check out the next page: *it's game-time.*

Author K. White (right) educates parents on sports concussions during a three part series on brain health open to 45 million viewers during May 2014.

Athlete Fast-Read Guide: Gray Highlight Chapters

CHAPTER FOUR

For Parents & Coaches

"I have been impressed with the urgency of doing.
Knowing is not enough; we must apply.
Being willing is not enough; we must do."
~ Leonardo da Vinci

On the matter of youth sports head injury, the U.S. stands on the verge of a public health crisis—joined by the rest of the world that participates more heavily in soccer, rugby, and competitive cycling. To be clear, this problem is best defined as youth sports-related brain damage from concussions, the accumulation of subconcussive impacts or blows (A-SCBs), and catastrophic head/neck trauma.

This position was officially confirmed October 30, 2013 by the government's collective healthcare brain trust when **The Institute of Medicine (IOM) and the National Research Foundation** jointly released the "*Youth Sports Concussion Committee Report*," which sounded the alarm that not nearly enough is being done to prevent brain damage from youth sports head injuries—damage that the IOM's eight-month "quiet but very intense" investigation revealed is much greater and longer-lasting than experts had imagined.[15]

When author Dr. Ashare was summoned by this IOM committee to provide expert helmet testimony (among his national volunteer safety duties, Dr. Ashare is the president of the Hockey Equipment Certification Council [HECC] and a director at the American Society for Testing and Materials [ASTM], which sets helmet standards) he said:

> *"Helmets in hockey are fairly optimized and only marginally help prevent concussions."*
>
> *The net translation: helmets do prevent skull fractures, reduce head-on "linear" concussions by about 20 percent, but don't help much with side-impact or mega-hit concussions (which cause multiple rotations of the brain back and forth inside the skull). Further, future helmet improvements will be limited, so this is not where most concussion risk reduction should focus.*

This comes from an MD physics expert pre- and post-medical school and former NASA fellow with twenty-five years of bench hockey team physician and national hockey safety committee experience. Lest one think that football helmets offer more concussion protection, last year I served on an expert panel set up by former New England Patriot ten-year veteran lineman Pete Brock with Dr. Bob Cantu, arguably football's leading concussion expert, who offered thoughts similar to the above on football helmets. More on helmets will be coming later.

When Dr. Ashare returned from Capitol Hill, I could tell he was troubled by his IOM experience, which gave him access to other national concussion expert researchers and their official IOM hearings. His concern was two-fold: 1) he had learned that concussive damage is more prevalent and severe than we knew, and 2) that the issue of accumulating subconcussive impacts for some youth may be as brain-damaging as concussions themselves. On the topic of accumulated subconcussive blows (A-SCBs), the IOM was presented with research on high school and college players that from pre- to postseason showed significant A-SCBs brain damage changes on new-tech imaging brain scans similar to those observed after concussions (along with cognitive declines).[1, 33] Leading-edge brain scan technology experts testified that soon-to-be published research showed similar A-SCBs damage in soccer and hockey players under twenty-one.[44] While we were well aware of A-SCBs, this IOM revelation stopped us in our tracks. There is much more to come on this in Chapter #7.

Brain In Play International's position is that this emerging public health crisis of youth sports head injuries can be minimized or powerfully offset if, in addition to the rule, equipment, and player, parent and coach education updates being put into place to help *make sports safer for youth athletes*, **_equal time is devoted to making players and their brains safer for sports._** Who will carry this flag? It will have to be the Big-3's parent and coach members. Perhaps the bond that will unite parents and coaches (traditionally not exactly close sports allies) is this book's youth brain performance enhancement innovation designed to protect and develop the brains of *child athletes that you both share together*. Important life-changing calls to action on behalf of youth have created stranger alliances.

This book focuses on what key youth sports stakeholders must learn and do now to protect and improve the safety and wellness of youth brains. We have identified up front that the primary sports stakeholders who deserve ongoing access and updates to the latest research and for whom this book is primarily intended, are players, parents, and coaches—or, once again, the Big-3 (led by players). In the world that is youth sports, these individuals comprise the day-to-day stakeholders for whom there are the most potential benefits and the biggest downsides from participating.

For parents, the brain injury dilemma is huge and complicated, but the good news you will learn many new strategies that can help to reduce sports brain injury risk and improve your child's academic and biopsychosocial life performance—the dream of every parent.

For youth coaches, the challenge can be less personal, but more complicated in certain ways, given that your prevention responsibilities center on concussion avoidance (of first and subsequent concussions) and limiting the frequency and intensity of A-SCBs. A coach's intervention responsibilities include recognition of potential concussions and fail-safe sideline assessment/intervention. The good news is that we have a new solution (called BPE-Youth) that aligns brain wellness and safety/culture strategies to help improve prevention and early recognition of sports head injuries—the ultimate for what's best for player injury prevention, and avoiding liability as a coach.

The additional good news for parents and coaches is that two exciting sciences are emerging informing ways to improve brain health by enhancing the functioning, preservation, and growth of brain cells. And that same DTI technology producing the ominous head injury news is also being used by bioscientists to link best brain wellness practices to improved brain structure and function. While BPE-Youth's initial draw for student athletes might be enhanced athletic performance and injury prevention (no athlete wants to lose a minute of playing time), the chief positive side effect is improved academic and psychosocial student performance—again, every parent and coach's dream.

As mentioned, increased brain wellness provides the best hedge to prevent, heal from, and avoid the longer-term consequences of sports head injuries—thus, the "helmet on the brain" concept. This requires a change in our traditional thinking, but it can happen, and it will make the biggest and quickest difference regarding youth sports head injuries—and that's all that matters! This will happen soonest in your corner of the world, nationally, and globally if players, parents, coaches, and providers can reach common cultural ground together. To this end, the authors will provide a model Code of Honor/Behavior for how this can happen—one that can work, based on having lived in this youth sports world as a player, parent, coach, provider and cultural change agent for more than five decades. We finish up this book with survival guides for each Big-3 group, including practical tips on how to combine newly learned brain wellness practices with those youth sports culture changes that together add up to Big-3 *'must-haves'*.

CHAPTER FIVE

Introduction:
What This Book is About
and Not About

*Either write something worth reading or do something
worth writing. ~ Benjamin Franklin*

This book walks what has become a very fine line between aggressively taking on the real dangers coming to light about youth contact sports brain injuries and advocating to preserve the extreme advantages that youth sports offers to those who play it—as well as those parents and coaches who supervise it. This line seems to be getting thinner every day with the emergence of groundbreaking brain imaging and analyses technologies (DTI Scans—explained in detail later) that show more clearly than ever the brain-damaging effects of both concussions and just one season of accumulated subconcussive impacts (A-SCBs). This is a fast-growing high profile challenge for all traditional contact sports, from football and rugby to hockey, soccer, lacrosse, as well as extreme and winter sports. President Obama's summit on youth sports concussions mentioned earlier, symbolizes the attention this issue is drawing. One wonders as a result of this White House Summit if First Lady Michelle Obama's interest in promoting healthy youth development through increased physical activity with her innovative initiative entitled **"Let's Move"** might someday be more aptly be renamed:

"Get Out and Play—But With Brain Safety
& Wellness in Mind 24/7!"

All this has not deterred us but instead has only served to create the ideal platform for an increased sense of urgency about how we can best and most quickly educate the Big-3 on sports brain injuries and the proactive brain wellness prevention steps that are part of BPE's Youth Fast Track Solution. This will support even larger numbers of Big-3 to be working together sooner to help prevent and heal head injuries by improving the functioning, preservation, and growth of youth athlete brains. Beyond the priority of brain injury prevention and healing, reiterating this premise also offers the Big-3 other major incentives, such as improving student access to athletic and academic performance enhancement, to re-mention a few.

While bad and shocking news sells big in the media, it is time for some good news that we can all collaborate around to make great news—especially given that the brains and lives of youth playing contact sports in America and around the world are at stake. Regardless of what neuroscience researchers uncover in the future, BPE's select collection of fast-track brain wellness best practices that healthy youth athletes can self-manage (supported by parents and coaches), combined with the principle of never playing head-hurt, will always *play* as an effective way to minimize sports head injuries.

This is why it is so important in this introduction to also emphasize BPE's concept of "activation"—the process that happens inside us when the light bulb goes off and we totally get the life-changing importance of an issue, and then change our behavior accordingly. We hope to accomplish activation for as many Big-3 as we can through the course of this book—for *players and coaches* especially in the chapter on youth sports culture change. We believe *most parents* will be fully activated to learn everything that BPE-Youth offers by mid-book—if they aren't already.

This formal introduction briefly outlines the major content of this book chapter by chapter. This will be particularly helpful for our busy middle/high school and college readers, as it allows them to pick and choose from some of the more elective chapters as described in the player preface. We will also be clear on what this book is not about.

This is not an in-depth book about concussion awareness, or a beginning level education. This has already been well covered by Chris Nowinski at Sports Legacy Institute (check out his excellent book *Head Games*)[16] and the Centers for Disease Control and Prevention website (www.CDC.Gov). This book is not about sideline and medical concussion management, as Drs. Bob Cantu, Jeff Kutcher, Chris Giza, William Meehan, Michael Collins, and others have written some fine books and medical journal articles covering these subject matters. Further, those American Academy of Neurology primers previously mentioned succinctly cover much of this territory as well for players, families, coaches and providers (available at www.aan.com or at Brain In Play International's site at www.BrainInPlay.com). This book discusses but is not about post-concussive return to school/play, which should be more aptly titled "return to life"—prioritizing transitions to family, academics and sports, in that order. Dr. Gerry Gioia and others have already written extensively about this important subject and created some excellent guidelines and tools.[17]

Before trending chapters, let's review Brain In Play International's major value interest which is **how to best improve and enhance brain health and functioning so that**:

1. The risk for brain damage from concussion and A-SCBs injuries is reduced up front;
2. Post-emergency concussion healing is of highest quality;
3. For youth suffering post-concussive syndrome athletes can build back brain cell wellness and functioning as quickly as possible (under MD or Licensed Independent Practitioner supervision);

4. Healthy post-concussed youth can reduce future concussion risk;
5. All youth athletes can leverage BPE-Youth as a best hedge to offset the potential for head injury's longer-term consequences;
6. Parents/Coaches become educated and activated Big-3 members;
7. The Big-3 led by players can spread the word about BPE-Youth!

Science is quickly catching up with youth sports head injuries, and it is time for the Big-3 to be brought on board with the latest. With knowledge being power, the chapters of this book have been organized such that the ominous news is up front, followed next by positive news—including encouraging science updates and effective brain wellness solutions—concluded by BPE Youth's suggested Code of Honor and Behavior that can help turn around the biggest head injury risk issue many Big-3 face daily—all led by youth athletes themselves supported by parents and coaches. A final set of brief chapters offers some priority survival guide suggestions for each of the Big-3 as their collective journey toward optimized youth brain wellness and safety proceeds. Here is a more specific outline.

Chapter 6 sums up the Institute of Medicine's October, 2013 report on youth concussions with editorial comment and provides a mini-update on the American Academy of Neurology's 2013 "Primers."

Chapter 7 details the latest research findings to improve the depth of the Big-3's brain injury and brain wellness knowledge base.

Chapter 8 offers six real-life case examples to expose readers to the range of tangible realities regarding youth sports head injuries.

Chapters 9-11 begins the Big-3's formal education about BPE-Youth Fast-Track. These chapters explain how we have much more control than we think over improving the health and functioning of our brain cells. We introduce two new sciences, *epigenetics and neuroplasticity*, break them down and show how the marriage of these sciences can influence quick and significant healthy brain changes that can help prevent and heal sports head injuries. Finally we target a big reason for BPE-Youth athlete buy-in: athletic performance enhancement.

Chapter 12 introduces BPE Youth's Code of Honor and Behavior for youth sports brain injury. The intention is to fine-tune the youth sports culture about sports head injuries quickly, without changing the great things about youth sports.

Chapter 13 details two programs preventing youth sports catastrophic injuries in ice hockey, and features how the **"Look-Up Line" and "Heads Up, Don't Duck"** together produce a more effective total strategy solution to reduce risk for paralysis, second impact syndrome, and severe concussions (than either does alone). The potential for both programs to apply their concepts to other youth sports is exciting.

Chapter 14 addresses sports head injury's long-term consequences. We share the evidence for repetitive sports head injury's long-term consequences and share our experiences attending pro athlete brain autopsies with Dr. Ann McKee at BU/Bedford VA's Brain Lab.

Chapters 15–17 provides youth sports head injury Survival Guides for each Big-3, suggesting practical takeaway tips and how the Big-3 can collaborate on key sports head injury priorities.

Chapters 18–19 offers call-to-action strategies and social media suggestions for both spreading the word about BPE Youth Fast Track and getting crowd-sourcing improvement input back to BIP International. We propose a future vision, which advocates increasingly active Big-3 participation in the space of youth sports head injuries.

In closing this introduction, let us once again give credit where credit is due and applaud the efforts of those thought leaders worldwide for the great work that has been done so far to help ***make sports games safer for players***, especially recent head injury prevention improvements involving rules, equipment, safety technologies and education/awareness advancements (see updates on Hit Counts and Head Sensors from SLI and Mom's Team, found at their respective websites). Let's also recognize those volunteers and medical/sports leaders that have enhanced in-game/practice sideline concussion management. There is no question that countless serious injuries are being better managed. We also want to celebrate the tireless proponents behind the **Lystedt Law** (mandates high school player/parent/coach concussion awareness and education and improved concussion evaluation and return to play standards), now operational in all fifty states.

We welcome the Big-3 to join us on a dynamic read of the rest of this book, which we hope will be a life-changing journey, focused on the shared priority of helping to prevent and heal youth sports head injuries. And we hope parents and coaches encourage the children you share to spread the word about this book's call to action, as well as joining Brain In Play International's campaign as adult ambassadors to make youth sports players and their brains safer for sports.

Women's Ice Hockey and Soccer are top ranked for concussions if rates are calculated per player, per hour a sport is practiced and played.

CHAPTER SIX

Institute of Medicine Summary

"Challenges are what makes life interesting and overcoming them is what makes life meaningful" – Joshua J. Marine

A surge this past decade in sports-related brain injuries suffered by young athletes prompted the **US Centers for Disease Control and Prevention (CDC) to issue a July, 2013,** *call to action* for immediate public policy changes. According to the CDC sports and recreation-related traumatic brain injuries in youth under nineteen years of age increased by 60 percent from 2001 to 2009 the overwhelming majority of which were concussions.[10] The CDC's timing to go higher profile about youth sports concussions was likely due to the concerning testimony and data being shared at the time by national experts before 2013's Institute of Medicine Committee on Sports-Related Concussion in Youth, (IOM) which lasted ten months. Amid much fanfare, in October of 2013, the IOM and National Research Council jointly issued a 306-page report (which also included testimony from military experts) entitled *"Sports-Related Concussion in Youth: Improving the Science, Changing the Culture."*[15]

The IOM's Youth Sports Concussion Report Bottom Lines: Youth sports head injuries are an impending public health crisis that all stakeholders must immediately take more responsibility for, including <u>players, parents, coaches</u>, thought leaders, and providers. Of note is that the Big-3 are specifically called out by the IOM.

The IOM's breakthrough discovery that did not get enough attention in the report's conclusions went public:

> It's not only sports concussions that cause white and gray matter brain damage, but the accumulation of subconcussive impacts that can add up over the course of just one typical high school and college sports season that now show up clearly on DTI brain scans of student athletes. DTIs are diffuse tensor imaging internal pictures of the brain that allow providers to see microscopic brain cell damage that does not show up on regular MRIs or CT scans/images. DTI scans and the associated new age analyses methods they support represent a new technology proving to be groundbreaking for sports head injuries— especially for youth concussions and subconcussive impacts.

The IOM's report was extremely helpful in beginning to get the word out to the public and providers about the total reality of sports head injuries, emphasis on the word *beginning*. The problem is if one talks with most parents and youth coaches, very few even know about this report, and there is no executive summary for players. This is unfortunate, as the IOM report is comprehensive and well referenced. That being said, it nevertheless documents the major concerns of national experts and serves as a validating reference guide for books such as this one (Google "IOM Youth Concussion Report 2013").

What the Big-3 should know about the IOM's key findings will now be reviewed, followed by a summary of what was reported in the major media outlets, along with an overall translation of both for practical Big-3 application. The upcoming 10-point synopsis will not be individually footnoted, as the relevant studies mentioned are footnoted later in this book.

1. Traumatic brain injury (overwhelming majority being concussions) will surpass many chronic diseases to become a leading cause of disability and death worldwide by 2020—with ten million people affected annually.
2. Post-concussion syndrome already is a top cause of disability in persons under forty-five and may become the leading cause in the U.S. by 2020.
3. The American Academy of Neurology (AAN), after extensive literature review, finds no firm evidence for reduced concussion risk for specific helmet brands/types, mouth guards, player positions, or soccer headgear.
4. Book second author Dr. Ashare, *"Heads Up—Don't Duck"* originator, Hockey Equipment Certification Council President, ASTM Director, testifies hockey helmets are fairly optimized.
5. AAN: The only evidence-based therapy to improve concussive outcomes is cognitive restructuring. Gradual return to play, prolonged cognitive rest and pharmacotherapy all demonstrate insufficient research evidence.
6. The only consistent clinical concussion outcome is variability in regards to risk, provider care, and clinical approach.
7. The "classic symptoms study" cited by most experts (a multicenter prospective five-year study of 16,624 college and high school athletes) finds 15 percent of concussed sports players demonstrate post-concussive symptoms.
8. Of the five million football players in the United States, 4.8 million are between ages six and eighteen, with younger age at time of concussion a primary risk factor for worse symptoms and prolonged recoveries.
9. Multiple controlled research studies report that gray and white matter brain damage occurs in high school and college football players from the span of just one pre- to postseason.
10. New DTI imaging scans/analytics confirm A-SCBs cause brain damage to youth football, soccer and hockey players.

While the public didn't seem too shaken about the IOM's youth sports head injury report, perhaps because they mistakenly thought it was about the professional sports world, or more likely missed it entirely, many in the youth sports leadership and provider ranks were surprised by the following sound-bites communicated point-blank in the national news across all major media outlets:

- ➢ Not enough is being done to stop concussions in young athletes.
- ➢ IOM confirms sports head injuries are major problem for both boys and girls.
- ➢ We stand on the verge of a public health crisis that the CDC warned the U.S. about in July 2013.
- ➢ Players, parents, and coaches are mainly at fault for not reporting concussions.
- ➢ High school youth are at double the risk for concussions versus college athletes.
- ➢ The youth sports culture stops injured players from accessing and completing needed care.
- ➢ The IOM confirms that many concussive youth sports injuries go unreported.
- ➢ Providers, parents, and coaches now know ignoring injuries could be deadly.

Many high profile news outlets documented the IOM's position that while sports equipment does not lower the risk for concussion, helmets do help prevent skull fractures, as well as spotlighting the IOM's admonishment of equipment manufacturers for falsely marketing that their products lower concussion risk—a reality consistent with the latest helmet information reported on later in this book.

Big-3 Take-aways:
1. Because concussion symptoms are vastly underreported by middle/high school and college players—*the scope of the youth sports head injury problem is much larger than what is being officially recognized—and perceived by the public.*

2. The most significant IOM Report achievement was to introduce and verify the reality of **accumulated subconcussive blows (A-SCBs).** While this greatly increases the breadth and scope of the sports head injury problem, it is what it is and may actually be a blessing in disguise.

3. If it not for a legitimate medical problem of extreme concern, the IOM would never have prioritized commissioning a ten-month special investigative committee. The bottom line is that we have a "tiger by the tail," and notice has been served.

Since we now know that A-SCBs cause brain damage on DTI scans similar to concussive DTI results, this begs the question for the urgent need to focus on *making players and their brains safer for sports.* This along with knowing most concussed youth playing head hurt supports BPE Youth Fast-Track as an absolute must-have.

In closing on the IOM Report, I would be remiss not to address the IOM's calling out of the Big-3. While there is no question there is enough blame to spread around to all youth sports head injury stakeholders, including the Big-3, given the growing enormity of scope and the embedded cultural tenets that have shaped this problem's rapid development, one must be careful to not "blame the victims".

First, regarding youth sports and the Big-3, most youth desperately want to play, most parents very much enjoy watching their children participate and are totally invested in their success, and the majority of coaches crave to manage their youth sports teams—most often for all of the right reasons. But nevertheless, when one does the emotional math here, it is clear that there is great potential for well-meaning mistakes to be made, especially given that most Big-3 are not knowledgeable about accumulated subconcussive blows, or the basics about brain health for that matter. The predominant culture of middle/high school and college sports is to play hard and win for your team, teammates, coaches, tradition (we must beat our big-time rivals), parents, self-pride, scholarship etc., regardless of what is said by sincere academic thought leaders who are quick to point out that the word "student" comes before "athlete." Try playing the card of electively sitting out as a precaution with a Division I college tight end, left wing, forward, point-guard or catcher on scholarship, especially if it involves a big in-conference game. It's just not very likely to happen, what with a band of talented freshmen ready to step up and take your starting position and a slew of national high school recruits just waiting to take one of those precious free rides (I experienced this first-hand with our oldest son on Division I scholarship with his teammates). And having coached middle school, high school, and college freshman athletes for many years, again the current youth sports culture is what it is: play if you possibly can—and it is very powerful, having been handed down from previous generations.

Despite what has been reported in the media and observable to most during fall and winter NFL/NHL games on TV regarding the dangers of concussion, again **most players, parents, and coaches haven't heard a formal mention about A-SCBs and some are even hearing to this day from many providers that most youth brains will fully heal from concussions in a matter of seven to ten days**—which patently hasn't been an advisable or evidence-based position to take with patients or families for some time now. This is not to indict those providers about such misinformation. It is, however, time to point out that the Big-3 (like most stakeholders) have been caught up in the vortex of what is best described as an evolving sociocultural, neuroscience research, and healthcare moving target.

It is this author's intension to extend the Big-3 a break regarding the IOM, educate them more fully, and provide tools that set the stage for fast-track change to prevent and heal youth sports brain injuries. We must focus all energy and resources on collaboration and getting into action instead of placing blame and having one more blue ribbon committee far from the action. The mantra of a youth coach from my past rings in my ears to this day: "Always forward, never back."

This IOM report summary may leave some Big-3 shocked and wondering what to do next and where to look for quick helpful references. It bears repeating that the American Academy of Neurology revised their youth sports concussion guidelines in March of 2013 and as part of this endeavor produced new sets of youth sports head injury primers. These primers are a series of evidence-based youth sports concussion guideline summaries for patients, parents, coaches/athletic trainers, and a great quick-check concussion assessment guide helpful to all, and more. They are available at www.AAN.com and there is a downloadable App that identifies and provides directions to the neurologist closest to you. The AAN website also includes a position statement on youth sports concussions that is well worth the read.

In closing, the IOM has released a bombshell of a report. The bad news is that *probably 90% of the Big-3 are unaware of it*. The good news is the report puts most all of the basic sports head injury cards on the table for all to see and reference (except the very latest research published since the IOM committee disbanded which we include in Chapter 7). The hearings the IOM conducted have caught the attention of key government officials and powerful policy and research agencies—which likely influenced the CDC to issue its call to action and use the phrase "emerging public health crisis". The IOM Report can be read in summary format or in its entirety for free at:
http://www.iom.edu/reports/2013/sports-related-concussions-in-youth-improving-the-science-changing-the-culture.aspx .

In this next chapter, we will zero in on the very latest neuroscience research updates since the official IOM report, provide understandable translations, and offer practical Big-3 tips and takeaways.

CHAPTER SEVEN

The New Youth Sports Head Injury Research Every Big-3 Must Know NOW

"We can easily forgive a child who is afraid of the dark; the real tragedy of life is when men are afraid of light." ~ Plato

Introduction: There have been so many important neuroscience research and news developments about youth sports head injuries over the last two years that it is hard to know where to start, what to include, and what to emphasize in our top ten research game changers. These final ten were selected based on what we think every player, parent, and youth sports coach (middle/high school through collegiate) should at least have a healthy awareness of and knowledge about.

I would have ideally wanted to know about this top ten list back when my five children played high-risk concussive sports every year in high school, before I was coaching multiple high-risk concussion sports, and prior to my own youth and adult sports concussions.

To clarify up front, concussive and subconcussive head injuries soon will be a major concern for nearly all youth sports. Research[18] confirms that some sports are much more high-risk than others for both U.S. high school and collegiate young men (football, ice-hockey, lacrosse, wrestling, and soccer) and women (soccer, ice-hockey, lacrosse, and basketball), while soccer, rugby and cycling present big challenges for the world's other youth athletes. Winter and extreme sports add to this high-risk mix for youth participants globally. But truth be known, concussions and A-SCBs happen in all sports.

Some readers may find these upcoming research updates anxiety provoking, but this book's authors are strong patient advocates. We believe it is the right of every player, parent, and coach to know the evidence-based risks of playing contact sports—*the other side of which is that, as this book progresses*, **the Big-3 will learn proven techniques that reduce these risks and help prevent, heal and avoid the long term consequences of head injuries**.

In the interest of transparency, the Big-3 should know that even among experts, there is disagreement about how some of these top ten research findings should be clinically interpreted, both in terms of how to translate them into day-to-day recommendations for player brain health and what they may mean for long-term consequences. Suffice it to say, one is safe to hedge their bets building on what many physician and clinician scientist head injury experts have already said:

"No evidence of head trauma is good for the brain."

To this I would add: **"The new DTI neuroimaging technology showing concussive damage to the brain's cellular network, including physical structures and physiology, and the uncovering of brain processes making up for this damage is not good news...but these same DTI scans have shown effectiveness of brain wellness best practices that unquestionably help improve the functioning, preservation and growth of brain cells!"**

In finishing this introduction, **knowledge is power** regarding **youth sports head injuries**. Sharing these Top-10 in understandable terms is important given the key stakeholders are players, parents, and coaches, in that order. This takes on increasing significance, as the change management scenarios necessary to successfully improve sports head injury's toughest challenges will require as many knowledgeable and motivated Big-3 as possible working together as a team. Not coincidently, leading us off on the Top-10 list is a reminder about how powerful the current youth sports culture is in supporting middle/high school and college youth to play while head hurt and hide their symptoms – despite all of the time and money recently spent on awareness and education. If this isn't a most compelling wake-up call for change going out to all who deeply care about youth athletes, their brains, and the sports they play, I'm not sure w*hat it will take!*

#1: As late as 2014, a majority of "concussion-educated" high school and college-age athletes admit they will play head-hurt and hide brain injury symptoms.

Many readers might find the above headline hard to believe, with all of the mandated youth sports concussion awareness and education now required in all fifty states due to the **Lystedt Law** (named after Zach Lystedt who survived second impact syndrome suffered during an 8th grade football game). This of course in addition to the mainstream media frenzy that continuously reminds athletes of all ages about the dangers of concussion. These perils include the showcasing of high-profile youth concussions causing prolonged post-concussion syndromes, permanent brain disability or death from second impact syndrome (a second concussion or series of A-SCBs closely following a previous concussion causing fatal brain swelling) or concussion-related clinical depression/suicides. The bottom line for the Big-3 is the ominous numbers behind the above-referenced youth athlete majority are comprised of your teammates, children, and players, respectively. So what is the research backup for this concern?

The Backup: In a confidential survey of high school football players presented at the *American Academy of Pediatrics Annual Meeting in May, 2013*, more than half reported that they would play with symptoms of concussion, despite being CDC-educated that playing head-hurt poses a much greater risk for more serious head injury and brain damage.[8] Incredibly enough, this study also found that those athletes who had more knowledge about concussions were not more likely to report their symptoms. In a similar study presented in 2012, more than half of the student respondents who reported having been concussed also admitted keeping their symptoms secret and playing despite having them.[9] Some relatively good news is that a majority of these 2012 survey respondents said they would report on a teammate if he or she was playing head-hurt. Some relatively bad news comes directly from the "horse's mouth" with a February 2014 PBS feature report that shows how powerful the culture of youth sports is over influencing high school athletes to play with concussive symptoms (i.e., student reports of dumbing down IMPACT return to play tests in order to play despite having symptoms, and pressure from coaches to return from concussions early).[19]

Lest one think concussion-trained college athletes are more likely to report symptoms, a recent NCAA survey found 43% of previously concussed athletes sharing that they had hidden concussion symptoms in order to stay in a game.[20] One major youth soccer study found that while almost two out of every three varsity players surveyed reported a history of concussion, more than 67% played with symptoms.[21] In a final sobering reality check, a recent survey with concussion-educated NFL players found 53%[22] admitting they didn't report concussion symptoms to avoid not playing—a finding only rivaled by a **2014 study on girl's middle school soccer reported in JAMA Pediatrics showing 58.6% playing with concussion symptoms, the majority of whom were never assessed by qualified medical provider.**[23]

I am compelled to say that I am not surprised by these results, which show that despite mandated awareness and education efforts, backed up by a great CDC website and a world-wide web of additional resources, the **majority of youth sports players are still placing themselves at grave risk for significant sports-related brain dam-**

age by playing head hurt. Professionally across a variety of settings, if I learned one thing about healthcare behavior change, it is that regardless of what the incentives are, *awareness and education alone are never enough to change the minds and behavior of individuals influenced by powerful cultures*—such as the one that shapes youth sports. This is verified by the IOM's recent youth concussion report, which calls for radical youth sports culture change[15].

One may think this issue is confounded and worsened by developmental challenges facing youth. My experience after spending a career clinically working with youth and coaching youth sports, says this is not the case. Young people are much less likely to be set in their ways and much more willing to consider healthy change, especially when being mentored by older youth or adults they trust. What usually is the case when talking failed change with youth or adult populations is the triple dynamic involving the absence of full disclosure about the need for change, not enough involvement in the change process and lack of communication—likely the biggest explanation for why kids are still playing head hurt and *a big reason for why we took the time to write this book (to help change this lose-lose-lose trifecta).*

Wrapping up Top 10 #1 let's recall that many Big-3, including players, have been exposed to "sports head injury misinformation" (i.e., just rest completely, as most youth brains will fully recover in seven to ten days or just a bit longer), the downside of which cannot be underestimated and has fueled the denial and minimization that underlies players keeping head injury symptoms secret and believing that playing head-hurt is okay. If you are one of the Big-3 that is nodding after reading this, just wait until you get to Top-10 update #4.

Take-aways

[Unless specifically designated, take-aways apply to all Big-3]

1. The rate or prevalence of youth sports concussions is largely underestimated, and we are therefore not even ballpark close to knowing what the real numbers are. **For the Big-3, suffice it to say that much larger numbers of our teammates, children, and players**

respectively are playing head-hurt right under our noses. Thus the Big-3 needs to be more hyper-vigilant than ever and not shy away from approaching players they have responsibility for about any head injury suspicions—be they teammates, our children, or our student athletes. Further, the Big-3 must be as open as possible to any and all logical alternatives offered to help turn this playing head-hurt problem around.

2. Concussion awareness and education initiatives are serving an important purpose, but we must do more of them and do them differently. We need to involve **youth** players much more in planning and delivering head injury awareness and education, to help advise on content and most especially to learn how to teach and deliver content—including participating in presenting it in some fashion.

3. Coaches: Watch your players "like hawks," especially any "usual head injury suspects," and have your assistants doing the same, especially during games. Evaluate your assistants carefully—if any assistant believes or acts like the sports head injury issue is being overemphasized confront him or her right away about what is an unacceptable bias, and unless that person convinces you otherwise, let him or her go. If an assistant does convince you to retain him or her, assign that person to read this book, starting with this chapter, and review it with them before the next practice or game. In changing cultures, actions speak louder than words, and keeping someone on a coaching staff that doesn't get it is just plain wrong. Also, keeping an assistant who is minimizing this issue presents a serious liability for you. While we have yet to see large-scale lawsuits, rest assured it is only a matter of time given what this new DTI research is bringing to light. See especially #4 takeaway next.

4. Coaches: While "when in doubt, sit 'em out" is catchy and has done a world of good, it needs to be reinforced in your head with the mantra, *"if there is even the remotest possibility that a concussive impact has happened, don't ever take a chance with a child's developing brain, because you just never know if or when a catastrophic downside looms around the corner."* If this sounds too long and dramatic, it is—but I guarantee you won't think it is too dramatic a few pages from now. I can't tell you how many times over the years I have seen coaches and parents riddled with guilt and second-guessing even their lower-risk decisions involving non-brain sports injuries with far less riding on the line.

5. Parents: **Watch your kids "like hawks."** If your son or daughter is playing a high-risk sport (especially football, hockey, soccer, girls' basketball, lacrosse, wrestling, rugby, etc.) and you can't be there, have a friend who "gets it" watching your kid(s) for you. Since you now know that most athletes will play hurt, it becomes primarily a parent and coach responsibility to be even more watchful. I can tell you from personal experience that the most committed coaching staffs can't see everything. And experience has taught us that seemingly minor falls and marginal impacts similar to those that may have routinely happened many times before without any harm can cause serious head trauma in perfect storm conditions. For example, Zach Lystedt's [Law] concussive impact did not at first catch the attention of coach or parent observers because it was like so many other impacts before that were non-injurious—yet it was the final straw in causing a second impact syndrome, and miraculously, though the child's life was saved, it caused permanent brain damage and significant disability. Coaches often stop watching kids after plays are over, and most will be observing players closest to the ball, puck, etc. These are not always where or when head injuries happen. In Chapter 8 you will learn about the case of my client Joe, a talented young varsity football player broadsided unexpectedly by a larger opposing player well after a play was whistled dead. While initially paralyzed from spinal shock, he recovered from his paralysis quickly but suffered for months from post-concussion syndrome, from a play that few even noticed!

6. Parents: Especially keep watching your children after games and contact practices into the evening if there has been a significant head or body impact (this includes heading a high velocity soccer ball) that may have quickly or violently moved the brain around inside the skull. And we are not just talking impacts that are head-on (called linear) but especially those involving hits coming from the side that cause the head to turn or twist—even from seemingly minor or moderate contact with someone's elbow or shoulder (this can cause a significant rotational sloshing of the brain around the inside of the skull). Caveats: remember that many youth soccer ball headers are equal to striking one's head on the windshield of a car hitting a pole traveling twenty-five miles an hour. One of our NFL clients only discovered his "decent" body hit during a practice that "rolled my head around because I didn't see it coming" was concussive when, hours later at home, he couldn't remember how to turn on his stove.

7. Players: Do not hold the confidence of, or keep the secret of, any teammates that are playing head-hurt. Report it to the coaching staff as soon as possible. Then it becomes the coach's responsibility—and that's where it belongs. For team captains, it is time to step up and **walk the talk** through leading by example. Don't ever play with symptoms that you think could be from a concussion—it could lead to a post-concussive syndrome that lasts months or years, or worse, sets you or a teammate up for catastrophic, permanent brain damage.

8. Coaches (and players): Reread #7 and make sure there is a "100% confidential concussion reporting policy" that mandates and supports all players to share concerns about teammates playing head-hurt. This zero tolerance policy is easily upheld when handled according to the military mantra: *we leave no one in danger or behind.* Knowing what researchers know (and you will know after reading the next several pages), having knowledge that someone is playing head-hurt and not reporting it is the equivalent of leaving a mate behind in a war zone—it is an accident waiting to happen that could result in more serious catastrophic injury. In fact, Chapter 12 takes this issue on directly—using BPE Youth's Code of Honor to mandate Big-3 behavior supportive of a brain injury prevention and intervention youth sports culture.

9. Players/parents: Playing for elite and travel teams that are costly and are not governed by interscholastic or NCAA regulations can be a highest-risk scenario for head injury because of the potential for variation in coach and referee preparation and the lack of accountability. There are two things you as an athlete should never put at risk in the following order: 1) your brain (because playing head-hurt can mean your life or short/long-term brain damage) and 2) your sports career (you do not want to risk more serious injury, and that's what is very likely "in the cards" from both additional subconcussive impacts and/or concussions). That these elite teams foster a higher level of competition between elite players, and greater political pressure on coaches to play certain players from parents is an understatement. There is oftentimes more pressure on elite team coaches to succeed in order to attract future players. The correct parental response is to not waiver in your expectations that these teams meet minimal standards involving concussion management. Offering to provide links for coaches to the American Academy of Neurology (AAN) website and/or providing copies of the AAN's best one-pagers for coaches

and other parents communicates a powerful message to elite coaches and may be more appreciated by them than one might think.

#2: DTIs will dramatically change the sports head injury world from youth sports to the pros.

Diffuse Tensor Imaging (DTI) brain scans are newer, more sophisticated MRI imaging studies and are changing the world of youth sports head injury as we know it—almost overnight. These scans allow researchers, clinician scientists, and care providers (if fortunate enough to have DTI access) to take pictures of concussive/A-SCBs' microscopic damage to brain cells that regular MRIs or CT scans don't show. DTIs also support enhanced research analysis methods to determine how concussive damage to the brain's structure (white and gray matter) is affecting brain functioning. While DTIs are not brand new, the technology/analytics supporting them has rapidly evolved.

DTIs following concussions and A-SCBs allow us to better:

- **Observe broken axons**—those long white matter neurons that are the brain's *communication cells*;
- **Measure structural changes** in white/gray matter; and
- **Assess brain neurophysiology** related to cognition (thinking), motor functions (movement), psychological/behavioral health (depression and emotional stability), coordination (proprioception), central nerves (vision and hearing), and integrative processes (all the brain's various cells, parts/regions and functions working together).

In short, DTI scans limit denial about the real consequences sports head injuries cause to the brain's cellular structure (size and density), and related physiology (operations and communication). Scientists have also improved DTI *analysis methods* regarding youth/adult sports-related brain damage, and learned both concussions and accumulated subconcussive impacts cause <u>greater and much long-</u>

er-lasting cellular brain damage than most experts had imagined, which is linked to declines in brain functioning.[24, 25]

All of this new DTI data is critically important for making better more informed decisions about the post-concussed student athlete's

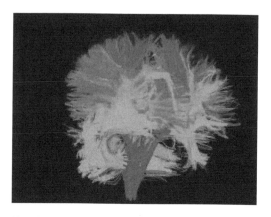

[2] DTI Scans show micro-cellular brain detail

return to the classroom and sports. Additionally, DTIs in combination with fMRIs explain why sports head injuries can be so subtle and hard to clinically assess, picturing damaged axons and gray matter getting compensatory help from other brain regions/cells[26], and showing how each concussed brain is unique[27], with highly specific damage that varies from patient to patient (explains why concussive symptoms and recoveries are so incredibly variable).

Take-aways:

1. The most important and obvious take-away for all of the Big-3 is to connect the dots between what these DTI brain studies are beginning to tell us, and the reality that the majority of youth players play head-hurt and do not report symptoms. Simply put, now we know for sure that youth who play hurt are gambling with their future brain health and that many players without symptoms who rush back to sports are participating in practices and games with brains that are still damaged and not functioning at their best (they may not have perceptible symptoms, but their cognitive test scores show decline, and DTIs would show significant white matter damage still present at four months – more on this coming up soon). An important point for all Big-3 to know and take to heart is that research has shown the most popular neuropsychological test used to determine readiness for return to play (called the IMPACT test) does not reliably pick up all of the brain damage changes that are clearly present on DTI scans.

2. To maintain balance regarding these early DTI findings, it is fair to say we don't yet completely understand all of the clinical translations of the images they are uncovering, and more research is needed.

3. The buzz about concussion and helmets in football, hockey, and other sports is hopefully dying down given the multiple studies that have been reported (most with football) that reinforce helmets offer little protection against concussive brain damage and even less (if any) for A-SCBs. This is because the cause of concussions is a rapid acceleration and deceleration of the soft brain that crashes against the hard skull housing it. Helmets just come along for the ride (see next).

#3: Today's helmets offer little concussion protection (20% with head-on impacts)—even less with side/rotational impacts.

Indeed, mostly what helmets do is come along for the ride when it comes to concussions. However, correct fitting helmets do a great job preventing skull fractures, what they were originally intended to do decades ago. This is not to say that helmets don't offer some concussive protection, but the most recent American Academy of Neurology analysis suggests they mostly help with head-on or linear impacts reducing the force of those hits by about 20%.[26] Helmets offer very little protection for side impacts, which cause the brain to rotate inside the skull, often causing more severe concussive symptoms and damage.

For the very latest on the biomechanics of concussion and helmets, author Dr. Ashare released in May of 2014 a peer reviewed selection of technical papers summarizing the findings of a national symposium he and Dr. Mariusz Ziejewski recently organized on the subject.[74]

In closing on helmets, let's recall the IOM's chiding of helmet manufacturers regarding unfounded claims to help reduce concussions. And Dr. Bob Cantu makes an additional important point—there is no evidence any of these add-on gadgets to helmets that are being peddled large-scale help improve helmet performance, regardless of what is being marketed—and warns parents and schools that modifications to helmets likely invalidates whatever warranty it comes with.

Take-aways:
1. Big-3 beware, as contrary to what anyone tells you, helmets offer very limited protection in preventing concussive brain damage and do next to nothing for reducing A-SCBs. Still, well-fitting helmets are vital to preventing skull fractures and do offer some protection in head-on impacts.
2. Those football players that might be prone to using the helmet as a way to administer a more punishing hit are increasing the potential for self-induced concussions and catastrophic head and neck injuries that can result in paralysis. In fact at the perfect angle of impact, any player crashing into another player or object head first has to only be traveling at walking speed to become paralyzed. Those hockey players who think helmets protect them while crashing into the boards head-first and duck down accordingly to avoid a face plant are among the sports players at highest risk for catastrophic head injury. In most cases, these types of head and neck injuries usually result in broken necks and permanent paralysis.

#4: Concussive brain damage is still present at four months—after concussion symptoms are long gone in most youth.

This research priority acknowledges the extreme value of DTI scans, but the research behind it deserves to be singled out. This recent study was conducted with ten-to-seventeen-year-old athletes, finding that **four months after concussions, when *symptoms* in all youths were resolved, DTI imaging scans showed structural white matter brain damage to still be present.**[19] **The brain damage in this youth cohort was greater than what had been previously observed on DTIs in concussed adults, suggesting youth brains may be more vulnerable to concussive injury.** This finding is contrary to what the Big-3 has long heard from many clinical providers—and seen in print for that matter, ***that most concussed youth brains are fully healed in seven to ten days.*** In a similar design DTI study with fifty concussed adults this same research group discovered **gray matter abnormalities on both sides of the frontal cortex of the brain** compared to healthy matched controls, again ***four months*** after a concussion.[30]

Take-aways:

1. This first study raises significant questions about when a single, seemingly uncomplicated concussion is safely healed, especially with regard to return to academics and sports. The DTI evidence of prolonged axon damage means brain communication is impaired. Dr. C. Giza, co-director of AAN's Sports Concussion Division and a youth national concussion expert, suggested the study helps us understand how developing brains respond to concussion and that more research is needed to see if this clinically translates to a more "prolonged recovery process" or "permanent brain changes."[31]

2. While the jury is still out on just how serious the findings of both referenced studies are, DTI evidence of white and gray matter damage that is still present four months following a concussion was a surprise finding for most sports head injury experts. This, coupled with the finding that younger brains showed greater degrees of axonal damage versus adults, is not good news—regardless of one's scientific bias or interpretation. Clearly, return to school and play decisions must now be even more carefully considered by the Big-3 and providers, and more research is absolutely called for.

3. The research in this area bears very close watching by the Big-3, as the key question is: "If a student athlete returns to class and is still having cognitive problems even though they "passed" the sports IMPACT test, doesn't this mean there is continued brain dysfunction?" The *question is rhetorical, and the obvious answer is yes.* IMPACT

expert Dr. Michael Collins would be the first to say: the IMPACT test is but only one tool upon which an MD/LIP should base return to classroom and sports decisions. The last thing anyone wants to be responsible for is returning an athlete to class or play before brain damage has resolved (exposing a child to more serious brain injury and academic failure).

#5: Subconcussive impacts cause brain damage, absent concussion, in high school and college-age players.

Multiple research studies confirm football, hockey, and soccer players of high school/college age without histories of concussion show evidence of brain damage from the accumulation of subconcussive blows (A-SCBs) from one season of routine game and practice contact play. **A recent study found six months was not long enough for A-SCBs brain damage to resolve on DTIs.**

One important 2013 DTI study[32] examined the brains of seventy-nine noncontact sports athletes, comparing them to eighty nonconcussed Division I college football and hockey players at both pre- and postseason to determine whether A-SCBs white matter brain damage occurs during a single contact sport season and how cognition (thinking) is affected. Contact players wore sophisticated head sensors to measure the frequency, intensity, and duration of acceleration of A-SCBs. *The study found significant white matter damage in the hockey and football player groups in five key parts of their brains compared to noncontact sports athletes.* Also of note was that the degree of white matter damage in contact athletes was directly tied to the number and intensity of A-SCBs head impacts as measured by their head sensors.

In March, 2013, Cleveland Clinic researchers had published a similarly designed study on college football players finding that A-SCBs indeed cause structural and functional brain damage absent concussion.[33] The forty players whose head sensors recorded the most intense A-SCBs had elevated blood levels of an antibody indicative of brain damage and performed less well on post-season cognitive testing.

In April, 2012, Purdue researchers released a two-year study of high school football players exposed to routine repetitive subconcussive blows during practices and games, reporting the majority of players exhibited cognitive deficits and structural brain changes from pre- to post season, confirmed by sophisticated imaging—even though the majority did not have concussions.[34] Another study presented at April 2014's American Association of Neurological Surgeons annual meeting confirmed similar results in high school football players.[35] *Finally, in a related compelling study investigating A-SCBs recovery, it was found that six months of off-season rest does not resolve A-SCBs damage in college athletes on repeat DTIs.[36]*

In all of these studies, A-SCBs damage was found to be cumulative, with severity of structural brain damage directly linked to the number and intensity of subconcussive blows players experienced. To reach these results, helmet sensor impact data from players was compared to pre and post-season brain scans, and cognitive testing performed before, during, and after season.

Take-Aways:

1. There can be no question that the primary take-away is that A-SCBs are becoming just as much of a legitimate youth sports head injury concern as concussions—across all major contact sports, especially football, hockey, and soccer (so much so that soccer has its own section of this chapter coming up next). **This means that youth contact sports practices must limit the number and intensity of subconcussive impacts on top of already limiting full contact due to its potential to reduce concussions.** Given this exploding area of neuroscience research, it is also good to have some developing guidelines for A-SCBs led by Chris Nowinski, Dr. Bob Cantu and Dr. Ann McKee at the Sports Legacy Institute who have been cautioning us about 'Hit Counts' for some time. **The A-SCBs issue is cumulative and therefore is a numbers game, and we must immediately start counting and limiting head hits.[37]**

2. Coaches/parents: There is huge variation in the coaching ranks regarding knowledge about A-SCBs in general and even within leagues despite standard trainings. Players and parents need to be prepared to speak up and educate about A-SCBs if any coaches or leagues seem

less knowledgeable than ideal or aren't walking the talk about modifying 'contact hits' as suggested above. It has been my experience that many coaches don't even know what A-SCBs are, so this takeaway may involve league officials inviting knowledgeable consultants in to help educate on realistic ways to reduce A-SCBs exposure.

3. Coaches need to adjust preseason and in-season practice games such that A-SCBs are limited. While some coaches may see this as overkill, *this is an issue of accumulation* both in terms of number and intensity of subconcussive mini-hits over the course of single seasons—which means they all add up to produce DTI brain scans that, if coaches saw, would change their minds about the importance of this immediately. Anyone who has coached high school or above knows that even practice games are super-competitive. If pitch counts happen with high school and college baseball players to save their arms, aren't their brains just as important?

4. We are early in our understanding of what these A-SCBs mean clinically. However, many studies indicate that absent concussion, cognitive test scores decline from pre- to post season, suggesting the damage that A-SCBs cause is cumulative and does impair clinical brain functioning. And the latest neuroscience on A-SCBs is even more ominous, highlighted in this chapter's Top 10, #9, which helps explain why some of these cognitive declines are happening.

#6: Youth soccer players are high risk for concussion and A-SCBs brain damage.

Some may be wondering why soccer is getting some preferential attention in the Top 10. It is because most assume football and hockey are the exclusive hotbeds of American youth sports head injury, which is not true. FIFA, soccer's international governing body reports 18 million people play soccer in the U.S. with 78% under age 18 (that's over 14 million youth soccer players, compared to 4.8 million under-18 football players).[38] And women's combined high school and college soccer is the top ranked sport for concussions over even football when calculated per player per hour that the sport is actually practiced and played. Accordingly there is a renewed research focus on soccer related brain injuries that merits the Big 3's special attention.

A 2014 study published in the medical journal *Brain Injury* examined most of the key soccer head injury research studies involving the world's most popular and fastest-growing sport, reporting that while 62.7 percent of varsity soccer players had a history of concussion, only 19 percent said they realized it at the time.[39] This study found that 81.8 percent of concussed soccer players had suffered two or more concussions, and we know from the NCAA's football study published in the American Medical Association's journal that being previously concussed greatly increases risk of future concussions.[40]

While those familiar with soccer know that most concussive head injuries result from player collisions with the ground and other players while running fast, head-to-head contact while attempting to head the ball in competitive situations probably follows closely behind, with recent DTI research also spotlighting the heading of soccer balls as a cause for concern (for both concussions and A-SCBs in youth).[41] Not surprisingly, the latest soccer concussion studies using advanced imaging found structural brain changes from concussions and A-SCBs, with heading the soccer ball implicated in significant short- and long-term cognitive impairments, depending on the frequency of heading the ball over time.[42] The Purdue University Neurotrauma Group, leaders in the study of youth sports A-SCBs, found soccer-playing high school girls without concussions demonstrated neurometabolic changes and cognitive brain declines over the course of a season similar to those observed with concussed athletes.[43] Yet another study on European soccer players whose average age was under 20 found significant structural white matter brain damage when compared to a control group of competitive swimmers.[44]

And we must recall the shocking 2014 published study on middle school girl soccer players, where 58.6% admitted playing with concussion symptoms—a study that also found that the majority of these concussed girls never got evaluated by a qualified medical provider!

While perhaps eye-opening to those who consider youth soccer a tamer game than football or hockey, the findings are not surprising to those sports concussion experts familiar with the game of under-21 soccer in America. Soccer in the United States starts getting much more competitive in the transition from middle to high school, with more player-to-player contact due to increasingly specialized scoring and defensive roles and "marking" defensive strategies. Players are bigger, stronger, and faster, goals are harder to come by, and there is increasing variation regarding size and skill of players. Soccer is the high school sport where fast little talented freshmen often compete against head-taller senior basketball team players playing soccer in the off-season to stay in shape as a cross-training option—both running at each other full-speed on uneven fields in inclement weather. And soccer in Europe and South America is considered a *way of life* with a more aggressive style of youth play that involves more headers and body contact at younger ages than American soccer.

In closing, I must confess that in my coaching career, girl's middle school youth soccer was my biggest challenge when it came to managing collisions, head injuries and rough play, followed closely by coaching a group of freshman girls in basketball. And anyone who knows will tell you, the group of boys I coached over the years in multiple contact sports up until many were college sophomores were as rough and tumble as they come, so what does that say about the head injury risks inherent in girl's youth sports?

[3] Youth sports head injuries are becoming a coach's biggest challenge.

Take-aways:

1. Youth soccer players are at greater risk for brain damage than previously thought, due to both concussions (most often from head-to-head contact and player to player/ground collisions) and A-SCBs (from fairly continuous body collisions and heading soccer balls).

2. A lower profile group of athletes that may bear much closer watching are girl soccer players generally, and middle school girl soccer players in particular. It bears repeating that when concussion rates are calculated on hours per player that a sport is actually played, girl's hockey and soccer land on top for across all sports, even beating out football and boys hockey and soccer. This means when you are watching a women's soccer or hockey game, you will more likely observe a concussion at those events versus many others.

3. While not backed up by research, anecdotally youth soccer players may be more at risk to be unaware than other athletes they have suffered a concussion and thus play through their symptoms. This may be due to the flow of the game (continuous running).

4. Heading soccer balls should be strictly limited to youth game situations if that, because of the high potential for head-to-head concussive collisions, and risk of concussions and A-SCBs from the ball-to-head contact. (i.e., heading soccer balls coming at high velocity courtesy of corner kicks).

#7: Concussed teenagers are three times more likely to suffer a major depression.

While not news to some brain/behavioral health concussion specialists given Chen's six year old study confirming depressed concussion patients have gray matter brain cell loss and neural deactivation in brain areas implicated in major depression, it continues to be a major surprise to the vast majority of sports stakeholders.[84] Still many others believe the low mood and sadness often present post-concussion can be improved if one wills it so or works harder to *keep their chin up*. Multiple research studies confirm this is all about biology, not will power. Regarding all middle-high school and college concussed athletes, concern about clinical depression needs to be high, as these are maturing brains, which for some may extend out until age

24, and potential for associated suicidal behavior is high. Research just published in the *Journal of Adolescent Health,* found concussed teens to be three times more likely to suffer depression than teens never having suffered a concussion.[46] Another study found 15 percent of youth with brain injuries or concussions were diagnosed as depressed, all things being equal, a 4.9-fold increase in the odds of depression.[47] Finally, a 2014 Canadian study found post-concussed youth much more likely than peers to be suicidal.[48]

These clinically concerning findings verify a growing body of literature and anecdotal cases linking sports head injuries with depression, as well as supporting the recent DTI brain scan research studies confirming both concussions and A-SCBs selectively damage brain regions known to influence emotions and mood stabilization.[45, 51] The Big-3 may also recall many high-profile cases of pro-athlete suicides, allegedly related to repetitive head trauma. The NFL's Junior Seau and Dave Duarson, as well as the NHL's Derek Boogaard come to mind. At a recent Sports Legacy Institute event Dr. Ashare and I attended in Washington, DC, honoring the life of former NFL Lineman Tom McHale (yet another multiply concussed suicide victim) we heard the mother of post-concussed adolescent suicide victim Daniel Brett speak eloquently about the need to talk more openly about post-concussion depression risk, especially involving younger athletes. This issue is of utmost concern to this book's three authors because we have seen clinical depression in youth overlooked and misdiagnosed so often through the years.

The silver lining in this particularly dark cloud of sports head injury is that depression is a treatable illness, with a recent breakthrough cognitive behavioral therapy study showing this treatment improved depression and post-traumatic stress disorder symptoms, as well as markedly increasing hippocampal brain cell volume.[49]

In closing, we would be remiss not to mention the strengthening link between head injury, post-traumatic stress (PTSD), and depression in the NFL/Military literature[50]—saying for now that Brain

In Play does not find it unusual for adolescents with post-concussion syndrome to also meet diagnostic criteria for both depression and PTSD. Finally, the Big-3 and providers (especially those without behavioral health training) are reminded concussive brain damage has been implicated in causing or worsening other serious mental health symptoms/conditions including those with psychotic features.

Take-aways
1. The Big-3 needs to know that depression is often part of the clinical outcome of suffering concussion that youth are very reluctant to talk about. For some youth, these depressions can be severe and engender suicidal thinking. While we need to learn more, what we do know is that depression is a treatable illness, and relationship-based psychotherapy often significantly helps—not just to treat symptoms, but also to improve brain cell functioning and growth.
2. Any parent that has a worry about post-concussive depression needs to act on it **immediately.** We recommend getting your child to a specialized mental health provider who you screen in advance by phone, making sure the physician/Licensed Independent Practitioner (LIP) won't be short-changing your appointment and/or leaving the psychotherapy to be handled by well-meaning healthcare providers without psychotherapeutic practice credentials.
3. The brain wellness best-practices included in BPE-Youth Fast Track were designed to help proactively address stress management and depression, and this is no coincidence. Middle/high school through college can be an emotionally charged time given all of the transitions and demands involved. Adding post concussive depression to this mix only heightens the value and need for such best-practices (see Chapter 11).

#8: Single concussions may cause persistent shrinkage and damage to key brain regions.

Outside of sports in the adult population, a 2013 breakthrough study utilizing sophisticated imaging scans reported that single concussions might cause persistent shrinkage to the brain as a whole, diminishing specific brain regions controlling memory, executive function, and mood regulation.[51] Such changes, including global brain atrophy, were measured in nineteen adult subjects *one full year after concussion*. Not surprisingly, brain regions associated with depression were particularly damaged, as were those involved with executive function (critical thinking), anxiety, and memory.

> *"Two of the brain regions affected were the anterior cingulate and the precuneal region," first author Dr. Lui said. "The anterior cingulate has been implicated in mood disorders including depression, and the precuneal region has a lot of different connections to areas of the brain responsible for executive function or higher-order thinking. This study confirms what we have long suspected [with concussions] is true [causing] structural injury to the brain, even though we don't see much on routine clinical imaging."*

Take-aways:
1. Since this study was performed on adults it must be cautiously interpreted. However, it is significant in that it sheds more confirmatory light that some of the brain damage that concussions cause is very selective and long-lasting – in this case, a year and counting.
2. The Big-3 is reminded (as are providers) that a lack of awareness or perception of concussion symptoms must never be equated with 'full brain recoveries' or lack/absence of ongoing structural brain damage.

#9: May 2014: A-SCBs implicated in shrinkage of key brain region in college football players without concussions—shrinkage of brain's hippocampus is worsened by concussion.

Just prior to this book going to press one of the most important contact sports brain research studies to date was published in the May 2014 edition of the Journal of the American Medical Association.[3] Researchers examined DTI brain images of college football players and divided them into two groups of twenty-five, those that never had a concussion (A-SCBs only) and those with a past history of concussion – and then selected a third control group of 25 college students who never played football for comparison purposes. What they found was shocking. The 'A-SCBs only' group averaged a 16% smaller hippocampal volume than the control group of students and the concussion groups' average hippocampal volume was about 25% smaller than the 'no football' controls. Additionally, the longer college athletes played football was linked to the degree of hippocampal shrinkage and reaction time deficits as measured by cognitive testing. *The brain's hippocampus regulates multiple emotional and cognitive processes and is the brain's memory and learning center.*

This study's findings, combined with the previous college hockey/football player study finding changes to five brain areas of players from one season of play from A-SCBs alone (one being the hippocampus), along with the DTI finding that six months isn't long enough for A-SCBs recovery, *is beyond concerning*.

Takeaways:
1. Some pundits quickly point out this study alone does not prove that playing football shrinks a critical part of the brain controlling memory and learning functions. However when you consider these results in the context of previous research on A-SCBs and concussion, and factor in this study's finding that 'the longer one plays the

smaller is the brain's hippocampus', this research is very concerning with regard to repetitive sports head trauma and strongly suggests a linkage. While we must be careful to not 'over interpret' these research findings, we must balance this caution by not responding like the 'Tobacco Executives' did in the face of growing evidence for not smoking, especially given the lack of informed consent for many youth playing contact sports under the ages of 18 or 21.

2. These results suggest high-school and college football athletes and other players of contact sports are high risk for A-SCBs and concussive brain damage (football, hockey, soccer, basketball-girls, and lacrosse to name a few) and would be wise to consider ways to improve brain cell wellness that drives hippocampal growth (refer to BPE-Youth Fast Track, Chapter 11).

3. See Top-10, #10 just below.

#10: Long-term consequences: CTE found in the brains of seventeen- to eighteen-year-old athletes.

In January 2013, the Boston University Medical School and Bedford VA Brain Lab announced that neuropathologist Dr. Ann McKee and her research team found Chronic Traumatic Encephalopathy or *CTE dementia in the brains of six deceased athletes who only played high-school football and nine who played football only through college.*[54] This suggests that significant and permanent brain cell damage from repetitive head trauma begins much earlier than previously suspected. One of these brains belonged to Eric Pelly, the 18 year old son of one of our advisors and another to 17 year old Nathan Stiles (see Chapter 8), both who died from second impact syndrome. In January of 2014, Dr. Ann McKee graciously invited this book's three authors to tour her Bedford VA and BU Medical School Brain Lab and stand shoulder to shoulder with her as she conducted two complete brain autopsies on deceased athletes to rule out CTE. I can only share that having experienced this, and seen CTE's distinct neuropathology under a microscope we are more dedicated than ever to reduce youth sports head injuries given the damage they can cause to young brains.

Takeaways:

1. The Big-3 needs to be up to speed on this issue, which is why anyone who knows that a youth player is about to play 'head-hurt' needs to step up and make sure anyone with active symptoms of a previous or current head injury sits out, it's just too risky and dangerous. **Chapter 13 provides a detailed overview of this issue for the Big-3.**

2. Providers and coaches (players and parents too) need to make sure there is a healthy margin or distance between when head injury symptoms resolve and when youth athletes return to play (further reinforced by the research previously documented in Top 10 #4).

3. That the seeds for long-term brain damage can take hold in such young athletes is likely explained by chronically inflamed brains which got that way from repetitive head trauma...this condition making brain cells, more vulnerable to injury and disease, on top of young brains being more injury-susceptible from due to not being fully developed. It also suggests that a genetic predisposition for brain injury/disease from repetitive head trauma may exist.

4. The issue raised by pundits who question the seriousness of youth brain injuries, is whether most of these head impacts (A-SCBs/concussions) are transient 7-10 day passing brain bumps, given their sometimes quickly resolving clinical symptoms for many athletes. Recall Top-10 #4's finding that while symptoms may not be readily apparent to many after a few weeks, significant white and gray matter damage is still present at the 4 month mark for youth and adults respectively. Thus the premise that a 'lack of recognizable symptoms' post-concussion suggests anyone can breathe easier about youth sports head injuries has been put to rest by the Top-10's #4, #5, #9 and #10 breakthrough updates. And we know A-SCBs alone with their unrecognizable symptoms are associated with significant structural and functional brain damage, which may very well contribute to the development of CTE as Dr. Ann McKee and her team suggests.[55]

Chapter Conclusion

There is no doubt the research involving youth sports head injuries and brain damage is growing more ominous day by day, making the need for injury prevention and brain improvement solutions supported by neuroscience more necessary and timely than ever. No longer are we wondering if damage lasting longer than 7-10 days really does happen with concussions and A-SCBs, as thanks to new DTI imaging and analysis methods we now have clear pictures showing measurable white and grey matter brain damage lasting at least months in youth populations (white damage which at the outset alarmingly appears more extensive in younger concussed brains versus adults). This helps explain declining student test scores observed after concussions and A-SCBs from pre- to post season, reminding us that sports related brain damage often causes both structural and functional (operating) brain changes that is associated with clinical impairment. And we also know that helmets, while helping prevent skull fractures, only slightly reduces concussion risk with hits that are head-on (called linear), and provide little or no protection with those side of the head impacts which can cause ongoing rotational brain 'sloshing' back and forth inside the skull (resulting in more serious concussions).

Most concerning, we also know that despite legally mandated head injury awareness and education programs now operational in all 50 states, **the majority of youth athletes report they will continue to play head-hurt and will not share symptoms with parents or coaches,** out of loyalty to teams or teammates, believing that 'gutting it out' is what is expected, or from fear of losing playing time to others, all of which are in lock-step with the current *youth sports culture.* Perhaps most telling for all of the Big-3 and the outside world is that in at least one study, **one's level of knowledge about sports head injury consequences did not improve the chances that a teen will not play head-hurt. This suggests awareness/education is not enough to change this potentially disabling or fatal dynamic.**

Finally, we learned brains are more vulnerable to long-term disease consequences and additional cell damage following concussion, confirming that once concussed, future concussions are much more likely. And regarding catastrophic injury, a concussion or a series of sub-concussive impacts following too soon after a previous concussion can cause *second impact syndrome* – acute brain swelling which can be fatal (read more about this in Chapters 8 and 13). We also forewarned the Big-3 about post concussive/A-SCBs related mental health short and long term outcomes from brain cell damage, including serious depression/suicidality and potential for psychosis.

The key question is, "With this youth head injury media/research swirl happening, what is the best position for Big-3 members to take?" After acknowledging researchers and clinician-scientists don't know the long-term clinical implications for many of these 'Top-10' up- dates, there are three things the Big-3 can rest assured about:

1. No serious head injury is good for any brain, and this includes concussions and A-SCBs...this being more true for any brain that has been previously injured;

2. The biggest day-to-day risk the Big-3 must take action on is preventing head-hurt athletes from ever playing in practices/games. Playing head hurt is a recipe for 'disaster', with potential for a catastrophic outcome;

3. A Big-3's best hedge is to learn all the basics about brain injury prevention and healing – including best- practices to avoid injury and improve brain wellness.

For now, the best middle of the road position is to keep reading. You will discover that these three above are truly where the action is at – and that **those best practices that improve brain wellness and healing are the same ones that reduce the risk of getting sports brain injuries upfront, and also that enhance athletic and academic performance**. How improved brain cell functioning, preservation and growth can be orchestrated to make these outcomes happen is de- scribed in Chapter 9. But first, this next chapter describes six real life youth sports head injury case scenarios which are presented to begin connecting research with reality.

CHAPTER EIGHT

Three Sons and Three Daughters

"If you look at what you have in life,
you'll always have more. If you look at what you
don't have in life, you'll never have enough."
~ Oprah Winfrey

This chapter helps bring to life many of the realities of the first seven chapters by describing the tangible details of six real life youth sports head injury cases. The chapter title was chosen because any of these six beloved athletes of caring parents and loving families could easily be one of our sons or daughters, brothers or sisters. While in the final analysis it matters not, I came to know them all in different ways. Nathan Stiles, Matt, Joe, Carla, Rox and Meghan Duggan are their names, of which the middle four are pseudo-names, for purposes of maintaining their confidentiality. While all are real life people and gave permission to go public with their sports head injury histories, only Nathan and Meghan's last names will be used because their concussion stories are already a matter of longstanding public record. After what has recently taken place in the public domain with Hillary Clinton's much publicized concussion, it is prudent going forward for all clinician-scientist writers to protect the confidentiality of their client-case examples. Of note is that I connected with Nathan Stile's father Ron because I wanted to learn more about Nathan's case and include his story in this book, and Meghan was the captain of the 2014 U.S. Olympic Silver Medal Winning Women's Ice-Hockey Team and a member of the 2013 Boston Blades professional women's hockey world champions, a team that Brain In Play International sponsors.

If not separated by the realities of geography and time, it is a lock they would have all been friends, these six hard-core youth athletes, three great young men and three exceptional young women, all of them at one time multisport high school athletes as quick to smile as they were to run off and compete in one of the games they loved to play with friends in a nearby neighborhood field, playground court, backyard rink or driveway. These six young athletes are all willing to teach the readers of this book whatever they can about sports head injuries so all Big-3 can benefit from their experiences, as perhaps above all other things, they are described by all who know them as good hearted and generous. And thank goodness for that, for as much as we can introduce the latest neuroscience research on these pages to back up both the 'bad' sports brain injury news, and the 'great' brain wellness prevention and healing updates, having some of 'both' come alive as true life scenarios on these pages makes it much more real.

The Players

Since I coached boys youth sports 75% of the time over my 2 decade coaching career, including national medal winning teams and D-1 college athletes, and managed the clinical brain/behavioral healthcare of innumerable youth players, I can tell you with certainty that these first three high-school male athletes all shared that special competitive fire that separates great youth sports players from the pack. Simply put, they live for and love to play sports and start out with things you just can't teach: speed, hand/foot-eye coordination, burning competitive spirit and brains that somehow automatically integrate all of these things. The sport and injury they all share in common is football and concussion, respectively. Interestingly enough football is a sport that while all played, it was not the sport any of them were most talented in.

Nathan Stiles: Nathan was a talented basketball player growing up in America's heartland attending a Kansas high school that generations of his family graduated from. Early on it was clear that this athletic and strong young man had a heart of gold, not being afraid to show public gestures of caring with senior citizens at church services, and gifted with a brain full of intelligence to go along with it. His 4.0 academic standing was balanced by his good nature and friendliness toward all others according to this handsome athlete's friends, many of whom likely voted him to win the coveted homecoming king award during his senior year. And he was a young man who from an early age read the bible daily and lived his life accordingly.

At the start of his senior year Nathan was excited to play football. The sport had not been kind to him delivering a broken collarbone his sophomore year and a broken hand after just starting practices his senior year. But high school for senior athletes is as much about hanging out and joining teams with longtime friends who decide together to play football their last year, as it is about calculus. At the homecoming game in which Nathan and his girlfriend were honored together as homecoming royalty and his first game back after breaking his hand, Nathan suffered a concussion. Neither Nathan nor his coaches realized it at the time and it was a few days later when Nathan reported his head hurting during the first full contact practice since the homecoming game that it was suspected he might have been concussed. A full workup at the area medical center didn't turn up anything suspicious, but Nathan's persistent headaches prompted a concussion diagnosis. This managed to keep him out of games for a few weeks, but Nathan reported the headaches went away and after the family MD ran him through a battery of tests Nathan was cleared to play. His mom Connie was worried but relented, thinking there were only two games left in the season and Nathan was symptom free and acing his schoolwork.

In the final game of the season, Nathan was having the football game of his life; one that seniors dream of as he was playing on offense and defense, scored two touchdowns and had gained over 100 yards before halftime. But just before halftime Nathan stumbled off the field and collapsed. He was airlifted to the nearest trauma center and underwent emergency neurosurgery. A second brain injury had happened during this game on the heels of a previous one that had not sufficiently healed which was major enough to cause second impact syndrome, that uncontrollable brain swelling that usually results in death. And in this case it killed a seventeen year old high school senior without a history of multiple concussions who days before was getting A's on high school calculus tests, and just hours before was running circles around the opposing football team.

In speaking with Nathan's father Ron, his son's sudden death took everyone totally by surprise and has had a major impact on the local community where this young man was an icon of goodness, faith and athletic prowess. Looking back there just wasn't any sign that terrible back-to-back brain injuries were about to happen to this strapping muscular boy nicknamed "superman". It was discovered that Nathan may have been taking non-steroidal anti-inflammatory medications in the weeks before his final game which increases the potential of brain bleeds in those suffering from a concussion. But from all indications Nathan was not symptomatic, unless he was medicating headache symptoms. In a moment of extreme generosity the Stiles family donated Nathan's brain for study at famed neuro-pathologist Dr. Ann McKee's Boston University/Bedford VA Hospital Brain Lab to be evaluated for signs of early chronic traumatic encephalopathy, the dementia that results from repetitive head trauma. And indeed it was discovered that Nathan Stiles at 17 would be the youngest athlete ever to be diagnosed with this disease. In a high-school student without multiple concussions, A-SCBs must be considered as a major contributing factor for Nathan's CTE, something that Dr. McKee and other experts have proposed is a likely cause of CTE pathology.

In my last conversation with Ron Stiles, he shared that while reliving the last few days and hours of Nathan's life, he discovered something of interest on Nathan's bible cell phone App. The last passage that Nathan had read on this App on the day of his death was a verse from Luke which reminds all who read it that no one is promised tomorrow, and thus to be prepared to live every day as if it might be your last. Ron was profoundly touched by this, as was I. From all accounts, Nathan Stiles had been living his life daily according to this philosophy for some time. And in recognition of this Nathan's parents Ron and Connie have chosen to celebrate his life with what is called the Nathan Project, where bibles are given out to those in need, over 8,000 to date. The Nathan Project also establishes nondenominational partnerships with religious organizations that commit to one year of bible study regardless of religious affiliation. They just need a desire to learn about what the bible teaches to qualify. Ron Stiles says his son Nathan would have wanted it to be just that way.

Matt: Matt's sports story entering high school is that of being an undersized basketball star – a point guard with unmatched intensity and speed, following a big shadow that has a way of getting cast in small communities by a 6'2" basketball star older brother who could jump through the roof, and was now on a D-1 pitching scholarship at the top baseball university in New England. Perhaps that is what drove Matt to play football so hard the coaches would stop practices to make an example of him, saying to other players that if everyone played that hard they would win every game (something Matt shied away from). While basketball was Matt's game he was becoming a freshman football icon – until he took such a hard body shot tackle from 2 oversized crosstown linebackers while running the ball during a late-season game he had to be helped to his feet, proceeding to walk over to the other team's huddle. More classic concussion symptoms immediately followed and he was removed from the game, never playing another down of organized football. After being quickly cleared to play, he declined to rejoin the team saying he didn't want to jeopardize his basketball career, when in fact it was later learned it was because he couldn't remember any of the plays, or keep much else straight for that matter. His parents also learned years later after this first concussion Matt could tell his brain was just never the same as it was before.

No one could quite ever put their finger on it but Matt seemed to change during this freshman year – family wrote it off to the trials and tribulations of adolescence. While academically his freshman year started with excellent grades, looking back, after his head injury they began to drop. Always an engaging young man with peers and teachers alike, his grades probably would have been even worse but teachers always gave him the benefit of the doubt. A few more official basketball-related concussions followed (and a bunch more on the side discovered later) and Matt's fun-loving personality changed to becoming more avoidant and less confident, with grades falling further, basketball skills and decisions becoming increasingly less impressive and risk-taking behavior on the rise. This natively intelligent young man was barely able to stay consistently organized enough to graduate from high school, but was cagey enough to hide his brain damage symptoms from 2 parents who were healthcare professionals, a raft of neuropsychologists evaluating him over the years, and a cadre of very sharp and caring high school teachers and coaches.

It's been nearly ten years since Matt's first concussion. In the last 2-3 years he has begun to share more about how powerful the high school culture of youth sports was to influence him to gut things out and keep his head injury symptoms secret. He just didn't want to disappoint coaches or appear anything less than the toughest guy around for his teammates by admitting symptoms, and was instead willing to accept the consequences of brain dysfunction. Not letting his parents or siblings know about his struggles with poor sleep, depression or disorganized and at times bizarre thinking, meant years of personal struggle and academic challenge before enough time passed for some healing to take hold. Matt now reports being so concerned about how crazy his thoughts were getting he dared not tell anyone for fear he would be locked up.

Not coincidentally as it turns out, it was only after Matt found himself in a healthier peer group espousing a healthier lifestyle before he began sensing his brain returning to normal. His old personality and organizational skills were coming back. In college he began excelling in academic situations and started winning leadership awards and earning the respect of school leaders. As he began endurance exercising and eating healthier his sleep and mood started to consistently improve. After attending technical school and finding mentor situations supporting his newfound brain/body wellness related concussion recovery, he graduated with honors and has relocated from the east coast to the west, working full time and living successfully on his own at 23 – at one time thought to be beyond his brain health capacity.

Matt will now tell you that his brain is much better than he can ever remember it being, but will also tell you that his sports head injury concerns are not over and probably never will be. He worries if his multiple concussions have set him up for CTE or early Alzheimer's like his grandmother had (since even though research on this has barely begun, early findings suggest Matt's fears have serious merit). He also knows he is very fortunate – lucky to not be brain disabled and to be alive, now that he knows more about the potential risks he was continuously taking playing sports while his brain was still injured.

Joe: When I first met Joe he was a 15-year-old honor roll multi-sport sport high-school talent enrolled at a small private prep school. Described by all as having speed to burn and enough spirit for 3 kids he continuously worked out to get stronger. He loved everything that playing football was about, from practices and the camaraderie of teammates, to the bragging-rights of being the heir apparent star middle linebacker from a small football school with a big reputation; that is except for one thing, the concussions. By the time our paths crossed he had suffered his 4th and this baseball star was being appropriately told by his neurologist that his football career was over. This last concussion was the result of a blind-sided hit after a play was whistled dead, which left him unable to move his lower limbs. Rushed to the local hospital, the good news was that his paralysis was temporary from what is called spinal shock from a direct blow to his spinal cord. The bad news was it marked the beginning of a severe post-concussion syndrome journey that featured severe depression.

To Joe and his family, this last concussion was straight from the depths of darkness. This was his fourth and head injury damage adds up. Joe's spinal shock symptoms reflected an impact forceful enough to cause major axonal shearing (meaning significant numbers of the brain's communication cells were broken in half), explained by the hit being unanticipated and coming from the back and side (causing multiple rotational traumas). This was combined with concussion's severe brain cell damaging neurometabolic cascade (which deprives the brain of oxygen and causes damaging calcium to flow into brain cells).

Joe's brain damage symptoms were of the 'classic 4' variety described on the CDC.Gov's concussion website (see 4 CDC categories and Joe's specific symptoms in parentheses below):

> ➢ Thinking (problems concentrating and remembering);
> ➢ Physical (chronic headache and extreme sensitivity to light and computer screens);
> ➢ Emotional/Mood (more intense and increasingly sad);
> ➢ Sleep Disorders (problems falling and staying asleep).

Joe being Joe, he was soon back at school after this 4th traumatic brain injury doing his best to survive in the classroom and attend football practices as a volunteer trainer's assistant out of loyalty to the team. This he did despite averaging 4-5 hours of sleep from staying up late struggling through assignments that he should have been excused from (with cases of extreme post-concussion syndrome cognitive rest is necessary for healing to proceed and Joe's school mandated the use of I-PADs, a notorious source of post-concussive painful light/vision stimulation). While the majority of Joe's teachers were supportive, a few weren't despite an official note from his neurologist excusing him from all assignments and prescribing any necessary accommodations. It was the same way with his coaches; despite the school being small, faith-based, and espousing a philosophy of deeply caring for others. It appeared those school personnel who were unsupportive just didn't understand that teenagers with multiple concussions are traumatic brain injury patients – which can, as the previous stories inform, result in disabling or deadly consequences. And what many don't realize is that the *cognitive rest that is necessary post-concussion is not only prescribed to facilitate healing, but also to prevent worsening of brain cell damage (something readers will soon learn more about).*

Besides the symptoms listed above which on a scale of 1-10 were 8+ by the time Joe's parents found BIP International, he was feeling quite isolated from most of his close friends whose lives were consumed with playing football. None of the well-meaning providers previously seen were behavioral health specialists so had not picked up on Joe's depression which was very severe. Joe's mom and dad sensed he needed something beyond treatment from a neurologist or sports medicine specialist, with dad saying, "It's almost like he needs paid friendship to help with his sadness from losing football." While the loss of football was part of the picture, Joe's brain injury was the primary cause of his increasing despair (Recall from Chapter #7 that concussion selectively damages parts of the brain involved with emotional control and mood stabilization). While Joe accepted that he had been seriously concussed, he saw his recovery as a competition he could master and have some needed sense of control over, since select cognitive and physical activities didn't worsen his symptoms.

In developing a treatment plan Joe's depression was managed as a priority, while at the same time we began teaching him the basics of our specialized concussion prevention and recovery program for youth called BPE-Youth Fast-Track to improve the functioning, preservation and growth of his brain cells—a perfect match given Joe's self-management potential. We counseled Joe/family to immediately scale back on any intense athletic workouts and to not ever engage in any activity that caused or worsened his post-concussive symptoms.

Core to jump-starting his depression recovery was spending an hour alone with Joe **right after his initial assessment** – this 1:1 meeting had to be exclusively about him and his concussion concerns from a bio-socio-emotional perspective. In one of the most exciting recent neuroscience discoveries, cognitive behavioral therapy has been shown to help accelerate the growth of hippocampal brain cells through developing a therapeutic relationship, which for medical buffs activates gene FKBP5[52] (significant given the revelation that A-SCBs and concussions may cause shrinkage to the brain's hippocampus by 16% and 25% respectively in young football players).[3]

Joe's depression responded very well to cognitive behavioral therapy and he absorbed the BPE Youth best practices approach like a sponge, quickly developing a sense he had some control over this "concussion nightmare" as he called it. Joe adjusted his workouts to be more endurance-like, known to activate genes which produce a substance some refer to as 'Fertilizer for the Brain' (see upcoming Chapter 11 on BPE Youth Fast-Track 24/7). Each successive week Joe showed measurable improvement (on SCAT assessments) and within six weeks most of his symptoms had resolved. Perhaps most importantly within a month his depression had lifted without meds. Joe's remaining challenges involve an unsupportive teacher and coach, but given his family's determination to sustain Joe through his recovery, it is unlikely these barriers to full healing will last for long.

Carla: It seemed like Carla was just special on the basketball court ever since day one. She might have been a bit of a peanut early on in those young girls development leagues but she was lightening quick, super-coordinated and incredibly strong. As she grew older she was becoming unstoppable, but more importantly because of her basketball IQ and point guard mentality, she was helping teammates to be unstoppable. By the 8th grade some were thinking this could be the next Sue Bird (U Conn/WNBA) in the making or perhaps the first female Alan Iverson-like talent. Most basketball gurus know this means championships in the making, particularly those from Carla's home state known as a national hotbed of basketball talent. By her high school freshman year it was a likely deal that a college scholarship was in the making; it was just a matter of where. It would be a just reward for all those hours of practice and giving up every week-end year round between middle-school, AAU and other leagues.

Only one month into Carla's high school career, this starting freshman's rising star suddenly and without warning literally fell to the ground, the result of a severe concussion suffered while holding her position to take an offensive charging foul from a huge opposing player. The head on collision was violent enough to cause a whip-lash contra-coup effect, which is when the head gets jolted so hard it goes back and forth like a bobble head doll. Unfortunately so does the brain also go back and forth several times crashing front and back against the hard skull, and often rotating around before the head's acceleration and deceleration is finally over. Typically with these concussions there is bruising on the front and back of the brain resulting in major axon breakage (the brain's longer communication cells) along with a brain cell damaging release of biochemicals. Out of the game to a hushed crowd came Carla once she was on her feet.

Unless you have met Carla, it's hard not to be surprised by what happened next. Despite being physically mauled by a much larger player moving at full speed and being in the midst of a developing traumatic brain injury, she talked herself and her coach into letting her back into the line-up in an effort to win a close game. Typical post-concussion syndrome symptoms followed (like Joe's classic 4 categories) but since Carla's parents were not at the game and she kept her symptoms secret, she went back to practice the next week. Three days later in practice her second concussive event occurred which landed her at the hospital, and while it is more than 12 years since that day, Carla's life, or more aptly brain, has never been the same.

To make a difficult story shorter, Carla's high school career was essentially the female version of Matt's previously described. Consistently minimizing the severity of most of her symptoms with others, she too was taken by parents to multiple neurologists primarily for her persistent headaches and became classified as a chronic pain patient. Her grades plummeted along with her bubbly personality, and depression symptoms, there since the beginning, were now worsening. Even though she was athletically a shadow of her former self, Carla kept playing basketball and softball in multiple leagues despite a persistent post-concussive syndrome. Struggling in most ways through high school and then college, things got so bad with depression she stopped socializing in college. She has tried every concussion treatment available including surgery, but continues to this day to have headaches and cognitive symptoms. But overall Carla is better and has found a job spreading awareness and education about concussions. She knows now that she shouldn't have played head hurt which worsened her condition over the years and knows she is lucky to have dodged concussion's often fatal second impact syndrome.

To close, Carla asked me to make sure I emphasized one thing above all others about her sports head injury experience, in true point guard fashion to help others of course. She wants all middle-high-school and college athletes (and all young women and men) to know major depression can be a big part of post-concussion syndromes and it's important to not keep that to oneself. As she mentioned this to me I could tangibly feel how deeply she suffered with this. She wants all kids to know it's just a biological thing that happens with head injuries, just like bleeding comes with lacerations. But just like bad cuts need care to avoid infection, Carla knows post-concussive depression needs treatment (cognitive behavioral therapy in the least). Despite her past challenges, Carla's personality is coming back full tilt and the world already is better for it.

Rox: A five minute interaction with Rox was all it would take. At close to six feet with an engaging personality once you got talking, it was clear from the start this young woman was going places. While freshman high school girls who grow this tall usually need some time for their sports coordination to set in that was not the case here. Incredibly smart and proportionately built, the first time I saw her play it looked like a college All-American was behind the plate in this fast-pitch softball game. There is no exaggeration here; Rox was the real deal and could have started on most college teams by the end of her freshman high school year. And this author-coach knows what he is talking about, as the softball team my daughter played on eventually won a national championship. Division I college recruitment calls started early, once she gave up basketball after her freshman year.

What most people didn't know is that in the 8th grade Rox suffered a concussion when she was hit on the side of the head with a pitch, leaving her with temporary hearing loss and post-concussion syndrome. She passed the IMPACT test and went back to school and played softball while still having symptoms (headaches, light sensitivity, computer blue-screen difficulties and trouble reading). Eventually these symptoms passed except for headaches. But there is no question Rox feels she went back to school and play too soon.

During her sophomore year a second concussion happened when Rox was accidently hit in the head by a swinging bat on the side of her head just above the ear. She remembers this as much worse than her first with severe headaches, major trouble reading and vertigo. Her parents were so concerned they took her back to a top trauma center for reevaluation but were told she was "just concussed". They did not take skull x-rays. Rox found herself retreating to dark rooms and just lying face down in the dark. A return to school was marked by several difficult moments of cognitive challenge (even though she had a neurologist's note directing her to be able to opt out of assignments, she recalls one teacher made her read a passage out loud which she completely bungled). Eventually it was discovered by a family MD, that Rox had significant skull trauma in addition to her concussion.

Once again looking back, Rox felt the return to school and play "happened too fast even though I wanted back".

During her junior year Rox collided with an infielder catching a pop-up and a glancing elbow to the forehead knocked her unconscious. Interestingly, her symptoms were not too bad this time and she only missed a few weeks before returning to play. The big Division I scholarship did happen, but Rox feels the concussions took away much of her athletic edge. It is four years since that last concussion but she still has residual vision problems and if she even slightly bumps her head or gets jostled, Rox gets "bad headaches that last for hours". She knows she went back to school and play too soon on all occasions, but was told it was her choice by the providers her parents sought concussion care from.

Brain In Play International has agreed to set Rox up with BPE-12 once she returns home from her college town and will suggest some interim best-practices she can begin to self-manage. Rox is truly as engaging a personality and athletic physical presence as ever, but I must share it was good to hear she has finally decided to hang her spikes up and forego her senior year of college softball. It's a great decision given the potential consequences involved should a next concussion happen any time soon. Rox may have lost a bit of her athletic edge, but still has wisdom beyond her years.

Meghan Duggan is a young women's hockey icon, dubbed recently as the toughest woman at the 2014 Winter Olympics where, as team USA's captain, she led the women's ice hockey team to a silver medal. When you talk to her she comes across anything but tough. In fact my wife and I on talking with Megan individually on two separate occasions both placed her in the category of being one of the nicest people we ever connected with. This after Meghan became an award winning 3 sport high school athlete at elite Cushing Academy and her University of Wisconsin college teams won three national women's ice hockey championships. That her professional ice hockey team took home the world championship in 2012 was just expected (The Boston Blades – Canadian Women's Hockey League). Meghan also won the Patty Kazmaier Award in 2011 as the nation's top collegiate women's hockey player, and was pronounced at that time as the best two-way women's hockey player in the world by former Olympian and Wisconsin Hockey Coach Mark Johnson.

In the fall of 2011 during an Olympic readiness practice, Meghan suffered what turned out to be a severe concussion, the result of a collision that in the process involved catching an elbow to the head. At the very time it happened she didn't completely realize it and played on (is this sounding familiar). Her previous experience with concussion suggested this wouldn't be such a big thing. It was six months later before she was cleared to play again, most of these months suffering from severe post-concussion syndrome, with early weeks on end spent in dark rooms. Back on the ice initially felt great but soon resulted in her severe post-concussive symptoms returning. The problem was her brain still wasn't fully healed after six months even though testing indicated otherwise, and with an increased activity her symptoms worsened again and persisted. In the late fall of 2012 out of desperation she sought help at Dr. Ted Carrick's clinic in Georgia where Sydney Crosby was successfully treated; Meghan says this was the healing difference that got her back on the ice during the winter of 2013 in time to resume 2014 Olympic training.

She feels lucky that she is back and has lingering concerns about her concussions, but wasn't going to let anything get in the way of competing in the Olympics and maintaining her aggressive style of play. Meghan has learned that every concussion is unique especially given this last one was so much worse than the one before it. She is a poster child for what can happen while playing head hurt even in the short term, as it could have ended her career, and as we now know could have cost Meghan her life if she caught an edge while skating after that concussive elbow when she initially continued to play. In talking about the future with authors Katharine and Bill White, Meghan is committed to getting the word out about youth sports head injuries, especially pertaining to women's ice hockey—and she wants to learn all she can about concussions and brain performance enhancement, to help others of course in true Meghan Duggan fashion.

Conclusion:

This set of six real life youth sports head injury cases were selected from recent clinical and coaching youth sports case examples because they represent the typical clinical range of ***serious youth sports head injury scenarios and consequences*** - starting with concussion's worst case outcome **second impact syndrome and CTE,** and extending to *persistent* post-concussive syndromes, including 2 classic cases of severe **post-concussion syndrome** marked by serious depression. The key questions that must be asked are what can we learn from these six scenarios and how can these types of sports head injuries be prevented, or better managed?

All but one of these case examples share one quintessentially most important thing in common: **All youth players returned to sports after concussion too soon or in other words, played head hurt!**
There can be no question that returning to school or play too soon after a concussion is a recipe for potential catastrophic disaster. Not only does this prevent optimal healing but in most cases further damage the brain. While a bit medically complex, the short-answer reason for never doing this is that playing head hurt exposes already injured brain cells to stress that causes additional chronic inflammation and the buildup of toxic oxidants, setting these precious cells up for increasing dysfunction and death—while greatly increasing their chances for future traumatic head injuries. For Nathan and Meghan, they played soon after their acute injuries, which in both cases severely worsened the initial damage done. In the cases of Matt, Carla and Rox, it is likely their brains are to this day still recovering from previous injuries, which were made worse to the point of becoming chronic by trying to continuously play through them. So again the point must be driven home: **concussive injuries NEVER stand alone, but are always complicated before, during and after**

by A-SCBs, and we now know these A-SCBs can be as brain damaging on DTIs as concussions themselves.

This reminds us of the research surveys on soccer, reporting that at the time of injury players often do not recognize a concussion had or was happening and continued to play. This last revelation is a most critical point for the Big-3's players and coaches. Most concussions are not events, but are processes where symptoms unfold over time, which is to say immediately following the initial concussive hit a player may not feel or outwardly show she/he is brain impaired. Yet ten, twenty or thirty minutes later they can't recall what day it is or what team they are playing, or in the case of our previously mentioned NFL client it was several hours before his classic concussion symptoms presented (forgetting how to use the stove).

The key takeaway for coaches (and players) is a compelling one: In situations where there is a mega impact to an athlete's head or body, sit that that player out for 20-30 minutes before making any decisions regardless of their current condition or intense desire to return to play. You may be saving a life or preventing a post-concussion lifelong nightmare—for real! In less severe scenarios, you might be lessening the intensity of a concussion and/or duration of a recovery.

The obvious point for youth athletes is that sitting out immediately in the short-term after a major head or body impact, or extending your concussion recovery time off a bit more in the long-term, greatly increases the chances you will not unknowingly play while head hurt. This in turn significantly improves your chances of fully healing your brain injury and getting back to your baseline of athletic and academic excellence sooner, so you have the best chance of performing at your best for the team, getting to the next level (should that be a goal) and returning successfully to school. In the case of Matt, Carla and Rox there is no question in my mind (or theirs') that their brain injuries significantly reduced their athletic performance in both the short and long terms. After reading this next chapter readers will have a better understanding for why this happens, but for now just realize that the brain is your on-board computer. It has influence over athletic functions far beyond coordination and instant decision making, including how the brain-body connection manages endurance, focus, the anticipation of head/body impacts and, just learned before going to press, it has a radar-like collision detection and avoidance system.[85]

So playing head hurt in the short term or chronically brain hurt sets one up to become less of an athlete than you were, or could have become, for a variety of reasons—to say nothing of the associated dangerous health consequences one is also gambling with.

COACHES and Parents: It is wrong to assume left to their own judgment, already brain damaged players can be reliably trusted to make sound decisions about return to school or sports or anything important for that matter – especially since we know decision making and judgment is one of the first brain functions impaired by head injuries. And many of these six player stories were negatively influenced by the culture of youth sports, which says 'gut it out, play hurt and don't complain' out of loyalty to team, teammates, coaches and schools. Turning these situations around therefore must fall to those who are closest to head hurt athletes who have first-hand knowledge about their head injury situations – and most importantly their current symptoms. Most often this means teammates, best friends and coaches. It can sometimes include parents, but as we now know, most youth athletes will go to great lengths to keep parents in the dark when it comes to sports head injuries. Stay tuned for the upcoming chapter on Code of Honor and Behavior for a solution that can quickly help address this.

Finally, all case scenarios were marked by some lack of knowledge related to youth sports brain injury awareness and education, in some cases by providers, educators and coaching figures charged with being supportive and providing guidance to these student athletes. Pointing this out is not to find fault but to emphasize this is still happening everyday involving people and organizations that one would think should know better by now (Joe's situation is ongoing as this book is being printed). This was most relevant to Rox/Joe's situations, where school teachers essentially ignored the medical recommendations from neurologists, thus exposing students to potentially more brain damaging cognitive hurdles. It is hard to believe that if either Rox or Joe showed up at school with a broken leg and a doctor's note excusing them from gym classes that a teacher would then ask them to run a short lap. Yet that is exactly the comparable situation that many of today's post-concussion syndrome children find themselves facing in schools, sports leagues or healthcare provider systems who have not completely educated or performance managed their employees about sports brain injuries. Stay tuned for upcoming chapters on the basics of youth sports brain injury prevention and recovery – and what you can do to help make a difference in this regard.

Bottom line Reality: Any of these six case scenarios could happen to probably any high school or college athlete. Because all youth brains are unique and every concussion is different, no one can ever know when the next tackle, hard cycling fall, heading of the ball, check into the boards or collision with an opposing player or the ground might begin a journey that plays out exactly like one of these case examples did. The great news that bears repeating is the 'same' neuroscience research bringing us the ominous brain injury updates, offers the world of youth sports a good-news solutions, including **BPE-Youth** - to help prevent sports head injuries and improve post-acute recoveries. The Big-3 must continuously warn themselves to never underestimate the power of the 'youth sports tough-guy/gal' culture to create bad head injury outcomes, or undervalue what a **Code of Honor and Behavior** can do to help prevent youth from playing head-hurt, and encourage treatment access and follow-up.

Some chapter ending pointers each case example verifies:

Nathan: One doesn't need a history of multiple concussions for **second impact syndrome** to happen. With catastrophic head injuries you can be acing calculus tests and having a career game one minute and fighting for your life the next.

Matt: His first serious **concussion did not involve a direct hit to the head** but a megahit to the body. Had Matt not walked to the wrong huddle what's to say he wouldn't have taken a bigger hit the next time he ran the ball (which would have been the very next play) and suffered a catastrophic injury? Matt reports with **all of his concussions that he never lost consciousness** – "I might have taken some good hits in basketball and football but I never passed out." In fact scientists are learning that being unconscious may protect the brain from damage in some cases and reduce concussion severity and recovery time.

Joe, Carla & Matt: Depression and other mental health problems are issues for many concussed youth (and athletes of any age). Second impact syndrome and paralysis are considered sports head injury's worst short term consequences, but that's because we haven't totally accepted the reality of depression and the suicidal thinking and behavior that comes with it, as well as other sports head injury mental health problems. Since we know that those brain parts selectively damaged by concussion also control mood/emotions, it is time to connect these dots. The great news is that we have some key interventions that help improve these same brain areas (they will be listed, along with the bioscience explanations showing how and why they work in Chapter 11 which breaks down BPE Youth in detail).

Rox: Softball isn't considered high-risk for concussion, but for women, softball, hockey, soccer and lacrosse have double the concussion rate than comparable men's sports based on hours per player that the sport is played. Whether due to less shock absorbing neck muscles or less quarts of circulating blood etc. matters not. **When we think con-**

cussions or head injuries we think boys and football/hockey, and when you do the math correctly that is not really the case!

Meghan: **World-class athletes (even the world's top female hockey player) can be unaware they have been concussed.** While this makes total brain sense, it is mentioned because coaches must be more aggressive to step in and replace players immediately whenever there is the remotest possibility a concussion has happened. Never has the phrase, "It's better to be safe than sorry" ever played better.

ALL: Hiding symptoms from parents/others is not all that hard to do—just ask Matt, Carla and Rox, or any athlete you know well!

In closing we must give special acknowledgment to the players and their families who graciously shared their head injury experiences in this chapter, so readers can best apply the information they are learning to real life situations. In no small way it is because of the many sports head injured youth and families who have shared their clinical experiences over the years that we now have enough real-life context to better understand the clinical implications of the neuroscience research in Chapters 7 and 11. Given this set-up, it's time to transition over to some solution focused chapters that offer more about what will help reduce the risks of, and heal youth sports head injuries.

USA Olympic Women's Hockey Captain Meghan Duggan and author Katharine White hug a few weeks before the U.S. wins the silver medal.

Good News About Youth Sports Head Injuries
- <u>BPE Helps Prevent & Heal Brain Injuries</u>
- <u>Enhances Athletic & Academic Performance</u>

"The only person you are destined to become
is the person you decide to be".
~ Ralph Waldo Emerson

After reading Chapter 6's Institute of Medicine Youth Concussion Report Summary and Chapter 7's worrisome Top-10 neuroscience updates, the title of this chapter probably sounds like science fiction! ***How can there be any good news* you ask?**

Rather than only focusing on the effects of traumatic impacts on the brain and its cells, Brain In Play International's clinician scientists also studied the latest neuroscience research developments on how to improve the functioning, preservation and growth of brain cells. We applied this learning to three-plus decades of clinical experience with brain physiology and mental health psychotherapy, and integrated it with a bioscience wellness approach based on Nobel Prize winning research. We have always been prevention and treatment-solution oriented (versus pathology) in our practices, and healthcare needs a balance of both. Author Dr. Ashare was introducing "Heads Up" prevention concepts as USA Hockey's national safety-committee director back in the early to mid-90s, *fifteen years before* most providers even knew about linear and rotational concussion models, and twenty years before the NFL implemented rule changes consistent with his original "Heads Up" premise.

The problem with most *out-of-the-box* ideas when first introduced is they are hard to believe and understand. The Brain Performance Enhancement solution we have mentioned to readers one-ups such thinking because it creates *an entirely new box*—a new brain wellness, injury prevention and healing system based on the latest principles of what is known to some as neuroepigenetic medicine, and two fairly new biosciences: epigenetics and neuroplasticity. This chapter will review our "new box" approach as briefly and simply as possible to assure basic understanding. Even though it's based on leading edge medicine, it sounds more complicated than it actually is.

[4] Improving youth sports head injury prevention/healing
means learning about the 'new brain health' biosciences

Epigenetics and Neuroplasticity
The Two Main 'Bio-Sciences' That Will Improve Youth Athlete Brain Health, Reduce Head Injuries and Help Save Youth Sports

The 2009 Nobel Prize for Medicine reintroduced a new science to healthcare's thought leading clinician-scientists. Called **Epigenetics (EpiG)**, it will someday be recognized as the healthcare discovery of our lifetimes. EpiG informs that the genes that determine our health (both 'good' disease and injury prevention genes, and 'bad' disease and injury causing genes) can be activated (turned on or up) or deactivated (turned off or down) by '*switches*' that control or regulate them called epigenomes.[71] It was but only a few years ago that if anyone dared to say such a thing, most scientists and physicians would have laughed them out of the room – well no one is laughing about '*genomics*' anymore. Googling 'epigenetics and brain' returns well over one million sites, which explains why the new leader of Medscape/Web MD is Dr. Eric Topol, a genomic medicine thought leader whose most recent claim to fame after being named the most influential physician executive in the U.S., is a "new box" initiative he calls *The Creative Destruction of Medicine* [as we know it].[72] BPE Youth shares Dr. Topol's "new box" bioscience foundation.

The real break-through discovery for humankind is that epigenomes take most of their elective marching orders on which genes to switch on (activate) or switch off (deactivate) from specific environmental exposures or behavior routines. Thus, the new rage in medical research is to find those precise exposures/behaviors that change gene expression, so injuries/diseases can be prevented, improved or cured.

For clinician-scientists dedicated to preventing/treating sports brain injuries, a related bioscience has emerged called **Neuroplasticity**, which informs how the brain's structure and functioning can be significantly and quickly changed (improved) in response to specific brain-cell friendly behavior routines – all happening because of **EpiG**, with many improvement outcomes traceable back to gene activation.

The marriage of **EpiG and Neuroplasticity** *means we can drill down to consistently improve brain cell health, resilience and functioning by targeting behaviors and exposures (best-practices) known to quickly and effectively increase brain cell functioning, preservation and growth, while eliminating behaviors and exposures that stimulate brain cell dysfunction, inhibit growth and lead to cell death.*

And regarding that "new box" thinking we just mentioned, this is exactly what BPE-Youth Fast-Track does.

So how does this translate to reduced risk for brain injury, improved healing of concussion/A-SCBs damaged brains, and avoiding long-term brain disease consequences? There are two ways this happens, and this is where it gets interesting for the Big-3.

- **Injury avoidance by enhancing athletic performance**
- **Increasing brain cell and total brain health/resilience**

Brain Injury Avoidance by Enhancing Athletic Performance

Put most simply, if an athlete can avoid or minimize a potential concussive collision or flurry of SCBs impacts in the first place, it logically follows that the concussive or sub-concussive brain effects will also be avoided or minimized. The odds of this happening are greatly increased if the athlete is as focused and brain sharp as possible, which as mentioned, is exactly what BPE Youth aims to do. This means a youth player's athletic brain-competencies are working at highest levels possible during games, including: concentration, visual-motor integration, instant decision making, reaction time, balance, emotional stability, endurance management, central nerves (eg., vision, hearing), and proprioception (complex coordination of moving one's body and limbs in space), to name a few. BPE Youth also supports all of these athletic brain competencies to be flawlessly working together in concert with each other as well, called integration. If all athletic brain functions are as optimized as possible, concussive impacts and A-SCB flurries are more easily avoided, and should they occur, will be more deftly managed by the brain (more on this later).

Perhaps most importantly, BPE Youth's brain-driven athletic performance enhancement also improves a complex neurological function called 'recognition awareness' (sensing that a big head or body impact/collision is about to occur, which enables players to best anticipate these mega-impacts and instantaneously respond). For reasons that neuroscientists don't fully understand enhancing this awareness factor alone significantly helps players to avoid the neurometabolic cascade and severe axon breakage that causes concussion's symptoms, even if this impact recognition happens at the very last one hundredth of a second. Our assumption is that highly sophisticated neurological processing simultaneously drives a youth player's last-second 'tensing up and shock absorption' to limit a concussive hit's damaging *bobble head doll* effect, which minimizes or prevents that previously described back and forth linear and/or side to side rotational brain sloshing, respectively.

Thus, what this athletic performance improvement best brain health outcome means for reducing concussive damage cannot be emphasized enough. The most classic high-profile examples might be the NFL's Tom Brady's and Peyton Manning's abilities to avoid concussions, despite being older, and less athletic or fleet of foot than they once were. If you watch them closely it is truly amazing how they seem to have eyes in the back of their heads, and how once they know they are going to get hit respond reflexively – and then walk away relatively unscathed time after time (and you know linebackers are coming after these guys as hard as they chase any quarterback).

Increased Brain Cell Resilience

The second premise involved with BPE-Youth's best-practices is that they ultimately reduce chronic brain cell inflammation and the build up inside of cells of what's called toxic oxidants, while boosting cell immunity. When you multiply this by 100 Billion plus cells it produces a more resilient brain. Inflammation is just a big word for swelling, some of which is actually healthy and part of a cell's short-term healing process. But when a cell is inflamed for a long time, its walls get thin and its internal operations begin shutting down. When you do the multiplication under these conditions, such a brain is more prone to get injured or diseased, and it logically follows this brain loses its edge in terms of being at its sharpest. Regarding BPE's injury prevention and healing premise, a more functional, cellular healthy and growing brain is more resistant to head trauma vulnerabilities (concussion/A-SCBs) and long-term consequences (CTE and AD), and if concussed, will likely heal faster with better quality.

To demonstrate the effect of chronic inflammation recently to 200 top coaches, we used an over-filled water balloon and squeezed one end to show how the swelling of a cell wall (balloon wall) makes it thinner and obviously more at risk and more likely to break on impact (so multiply this by 100 Billion plus – and you will no longer wonder why those with a history of concussion are much more likely to have others, because with concussions and flurries of A-SCBs, so also comes chronic inflammation and less resilient cells).

Toxic oxidant buildup in brain cells (from trauma, unhealthy behavior, inflammation) is dangerous because it makes cells less functional, causes more inflammation, and accelerates cell aging/death (that's why blueberries and omega-3 fats are good for the brain – they are powerful antioxidants). Thinking of fruit, consider two peaches, one just before ripening with its cells firm and at the top of their game, and another that is overly ripened. How do you think each would fare if dropped onto a hard surface 5 times? I'm betting the peach with the least amount of cell inflammation and oxidants will survive those five impacts in better shape, and we all know which one that is.

Youth sports brain injury and disease 'prevention and healing' therefore involves identifying and implementing those exposures and behaviors that turn on/up 'good' genes that will improve brain cell functioning, preservation and growth, and avoiding at all costs those known to activate 'bad' genes that will cause cell dysfunction, chronic inflammation and oxidant buildup. As you will learn in the next few chapters, BPE-Youth Fast-Track helps orchestrate this to happen, thanks to that marriage of Epi-G and Neuroplasticity

Quick Read Summary- Bottom Line for Now: To prevent and best heal brain injuries, we want to do whatever we can to increase and then maintain the health and resilience of our brain cells, both as individual cells and as an organ collection of 100 billion-plus thinking and communicating neurons that make up our brains. We always want youth athlete brain cells to be working at top capacity but especially so during practices and games so they can make best decisions, maintain top awareness/avoidance for high risk impact situations, perform and anticipate making complex athletic moves to adjust to those big hits about to happen etcetera. The Big-3 wants youth brains (cells) to avoid chronic inflammation and the build-up of toxins – both caused and worsened by lifestyles that have unhealthy behaviors (such as eating fried or high sugar foods, not getting enough sleep, drinking alcoholic beverages etc.) and a lack of brain wellness habits. Those with concussion histories are at highest risk. The Big-3 wants every youth brain cell functioning at top levels and each cell membrane wall as strong as possible. As the cliché says, just do the math!

In the next chapter, the reader will come to understand how this all works in a more detailed way...and that we have considerable control over the performance and resilience of our brains. For now just realize that the state of wellness of one's brain:

1. Influences all athletic brain functions during games/practices, such as: cognitive (thinking), emotional (intensity), motor (movement), central nerve (vision/hearing) and integrative (how all brain parts/functions work together). Games and contact practices are when concussion risk is highest!

2. Directly ties 1:1 to the condition of an athlete's brain cells [top brain cell wellness means brain cells avoid inflammation and the build-up of toxins, and if this can be orchestrated to happen our brains are much less likely to get injured from trauma].

In closing this chapter, we want to emphasize a core concept the Big-3 will be reading about over and over regarding all that has been introduced in this chapter – ***The Brain Is In Play 24/7.***

When coaches say championships are won well before the final tournament games are played, whether all coaches fully realize it or not they are not just referring to traditional physical and psychological preparation, but brain wellness-readiness also – going far beyond what is traditionally thought as mental preparation. Mental prep is typically thought of as a state of mind associated with the will to win, and belief in self and team. What we are talking about here involves the brain (and its cells) organizing and influencing all things – from focus and endurance to actual game performance. We are also learning that much of physical preparation is controlled, coordinated and integrated by the brain 24/7. It might be hard for some to believe that a few poor nights of sleep and some evenings of excessive beer drinking a few days before a game, combined with poor hydration prep and a bad pregame meal can determine the outcome of a championship game. But it's true, and happens all of the time. For some athletes it can even mean the difference between getting a significant head injury or not.

Can you imagine a youth sports world where the worry about sports related concussions and other head injuries wanes, and the rate of head injuries begins to fall dramatically? And those with persistent post-concussion syndrome start reporting getting better faster, benefiting from reliable self-management options under the supervision of their credentialed medical providers. This is where your book journey travels next.

CHAPTER TEN

The Brain Performance Enhancement System^{sm}

"Strive not to be a success, but rather to be of value"

~ Albert Einstein

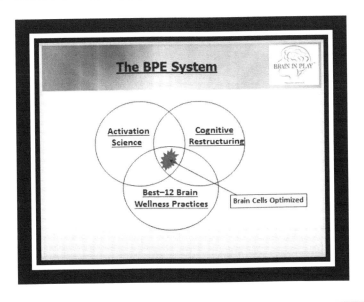

Brain In Play International's original patent-pending brain wellness system helps prevent and heal brain injuries and diseases and is called Brain Performance Enhancement^{sm} (see above). Called BPE-12 for short, it optimizes the functioning, preservation and growth of brain cells by combining 12 brain wellness best practices, which are jump-started by an activation science and sustained by cognitive therapy.

BPE Youth Fast-Track is a condensed version of BPE-12 created for youth athletes, which is described in detail in Chapter eleven. Called BPE Youth for short it utilizes six of BPE-12's best practices and two activation science concepts from the original model to improve the functioning, preservation and growth of brain cells. Its primary purpose is to provide youth with behavioral protocols that:

1. Reduces head injury risk factors upfront;
2. Helps prevent or offset the A-SCBs factor;
3. Enhances the recovery process from concussions;
4. Helps youth with concussion histories avoid repeat concussions;
5. Prevents head hurt athletes from ever playing while injured.

BPE-Youth also enhances athletic and academic performance, exciting collateral effects all Big-3 will come to appreciate. This chapter briefly describes the original BPE-12 system which has been prototyped with world class athletes, high school age through the professional ranks, so readers can better understand how a fast-track version for youth adds extreme value to the youth sports head injury prevention, healing and consequence avoidance challenge.

BPE-12 is a three part brain wellness system which helps prevent and heal the brain damage from concussions and A-SCBs by creating the strongest and highest functioning collection of cells possible that make up an athlete's brain. As chapter nine outlined, this happens by adding best-practice behavior routines that produce healthiest brain-cells, in tandem with eliminating unhealthy behaviors that activate 'bad gene' expression making brains more vulnerable to injuries and diseases (thanks to how the sciences of epigenetics and neuroplasticity can be manipulated). This ultimately creates a top living environment for brain cells, optimizing their functioning, preservation and growth. The BPE-12 system is comprised of the following 3 components:

1. 12 Brain Wellness Best-Practices: A targeted group of environmental enrichment, behavioral management and brain stimulation techniques, eight of which enhance brain functioning and structure;

2. 10-Point Activation Science: A unique set of client/patient activators which powerfully engages and strongly motivates commitment to the 'Best-12' (hardwires a blueprint for behavior-change success);

3. Cognitive Behavioral Restructuring: An evidence-based formal therapy helping clients best manage thoughts, actions and feelings which sustains Best-12 adherence AND improves brain cell functioning and growth (hippocampus).[49]

Many of BPE-12's best-practices can be traced back to changing the expression of specific genes, so switching on multiple good gene expressions 24/7 (while simultaneously turning off bad ones) produces the healthiest most resilient group of brain cells possible. A similar injury/disease prevention paradigm earned the 2009 Nobel Prize in medicine. BIP International has applied this Nobel principle to produce stronger, more functional and cellular-healthy brains that are more resilient and resistant to injury and illness vulnerability in the first place. Such healthiest brains are also best prepared to facilitate healing in the event of concussive trauma.

In the world of sports BPE-12 is used for:

➢ **Prevention-maintenance**: For athletes to reduce concussion risk to a bare minimum (most critical the year after a concussion when risk is greatest and during the off-season to build back brain cell health compromised by A-SCBs);

➢ **Therapeutic healing**: Following concussion to improve the quality of recovery (for accelerated and improved brain cell functioning, preservation and growth). This use requires the supervision of an MD or

Licensed Independent Practitioner board certified in behavioral/brain health;

➢ **Performance Enhancement**: For the ultimate world class athletic edge, as healthiest athletic brain = best performance;

➢ **Best hedge therapy**: To prevent or ameliorate repetitive head injury-related, and age-related, chronic brain diseases.

As mentioned, **BPE Youth Fast-Track** is a mini-version of BPE-12 designed for the day-to-day benefit of middle/high-school and college players. How can each Big-3 group use this innovation to best prevent/heal sports head injuries?

For Players: The key is to commit to BPE's Youth Fast Track Program that you will learn about in the next chapter, and follow as closely as possible as many of the six select best brain wellness practices as you can. Try as many as are doable and see how much better you feel (as what enhances your brain functioning quickly improves your mood, sense of clarity and focus). Then go one step further, and embrace BPE's Honor Code (code of honor and behavior that prevents you and your teammates from playing head-hurt). Then think about going a final step further, to help pay forward BPE Youth to others, which you will learn how to do in Chapter 18. The reason for all of this is to make your brain and the brains of others safer for sports, while boosting athletic and academic performance.

For Parents: Learn BPE's Youth Fast-Track Program and support player adherence by making it easier for players to sustain brain healthy choices over time. Consider getting brain-healthy yourself by following some or all of the six best brain wellness practices. This provides a great example for your student athlete(s), and you will feel better and slow down your aging at the same time (also food shopping will be easier). Also support chapter twelve's BPE Code of Honor and Behavior – so your son or daughter never gambles with their brain or life by playing head-hurt (it also helps make the other Big-3 parties more accountable as well). Learning BPE Youth and its Honor Code will help in ways that are unimaginable, and may even save a life from preventing a second impact syndrome or a suicide from a post-concussive/A-SCBs major depression.

For Coaches: Learn, reinforce and integrate as many of BPE's Fast-Track best routines as possible into your practices and mentoring situations (we will show you an easy way to do this). Coach and educate players and parents on the direct connection between brain wellness and injury prevention/healing, as well as best athletic and academic performance. Coaches are the backbone of any successful culture change, so totally embrace BPE Youth's Code of Honor and Behavior – you will definitely improve and potentially save lives. And you will be spreading out the responsibility and accountability for not playing head hurt by involving players and parents.

The next several chapters will show the Big-3 how to make all of this happen, one threesome, team, league, school or organization at a time, further broken down by Big-3 role in upcoming survival guide chapters.

CHAPTER ELEVEN

BPE Youth Fast-Track^{sm}

If you're offered a ride on a rocket ship, don't ask what seat!
Just get on. ~ Sheryl Sandberg

BPE Youth Fast-Track^{sm} (BPE Youth) is a condensed version of the original Brain Performance Enhancement^{sm} or BPE-12 system designed for middle/high-school and college athletes to help prevent, heal and **avoid the longer-term consequences** of sports head injuries, **including concussions, A-SCBs and catastrophic events**. BPE Youth extracts and customizes six of BPE-12's original top brain wellness best practices along with two key behavior activators from the original patent pending brain wellness system to jump-start youth athletes to reduce sports head injuries and their after-effects.

We want to remind all Big-3 that while sports head injury prevention, healing and consequence avoidance are the primary reasons for BPE Youth Fast-Track, athletic and academic performance enhancement are also major intended outcomes.

To help the Big-3 learn and transition to this fast-track program, the acronym '**BE CHAMPS - 24/7**' was developed as a helpful teaching tool and reminder for BPE Youth's six best brain wellness practices and two activators. Blended together these best-practices and activators were selected to quickly optimize brain cell operations and resilience (brain injury prevention) while also improving brain cell functioning, preservation and growth (injury healing and disease consequence-avoidance). BPE Youth's ultimate goal is to **REMOVE** the 'behaviors' that cause brain cell inflammation and toxic oxidant build-up, and **ADD** behavior-routines producing top brain cell functioning and growth. To powerfully engage and sustain youth in brain-optimized lifestyle behaviors two main activators are introduced, the Honor Code and planning/tracking progress.

The 24/7 acronym add-on emphasizes the brain's around the clock continuity (we may sleep but the brain keeps functioning). The 24/7 element reinforces that whatever behavior(s) a player engages in the night before, or even days in advance of a game, can and does influence game performance, and may spell the difference between an injury happening or not, its severity, and its healing speed/capacity.

BPE Youth Fast-Track: BE CHAMPS - 24/7

B – Breathing to Focus: Improves brain structure and functions;
E – Exercise: Increases brain volume (memory and learning);

C – Cortisol/Stress Reduction: Boosts brain wellness/growth
H – *Honor/Behavior Code: To prevent playing while head-hurt
A – Auto-Regulation: Biology for sleep, hydration and muscles
M –Meals Change Brains: Eating smart improves brain cells
P – *Planning: Plan & Track up to 6 daily routines for success
S – Substances: May 2014 - Alcohol/Marijuana = brain damage

24/7: The Brain is in Play 24 hours a day and 7 days a week – Always.

*Refers to a Behavior/Motivation Activator

The Big-3 might be asking two questions: "Why more than 2or 3 best practices and why activators for behavior-routines?"

First, combining multiple best brain wellness practices ensures switching on and turning up the expression of as many good genes as possible that will facilitate top brain cell functioning, preservation and growth, while switching off or turning down the expression of as many potential high-risk bad genes known to have the opposite effect (causing brain cell dysfunction or damage). Also, not all youth brains respond exactly the same to specific best practices – for example some athletes may respond more favorably than others to gene-expressions stimulated by the combo of *exercise and meals that are brain-smart*, versus others who may be more reactive to *'breathing' and sleep improvement* instead. Thus, having a range/group of key best practices known to positively activate gene expression in most individuals simply increases the odds that all youth brains can leverage the BPE Youth Fast Track System (so that neuroplasticity in terms of driving both brain cell growth and functioning/communication improvements happens quickly). While far beyond the scope of this book, variable athlete responses to given best practices is genetically determined, so this aggregate approach really does improve likelihood for success.

Second, scientists have recently learned that in cases of new brain cell development (produced by endurance exercise for example), such new growth must be accompanied by additional forms of brain wellness stimulation such as new behavior or learning in order for new brain cells to endure to maturity.[56] To cover this base we have aggregated or grouped key select best-practices that help make this happen as a matter of course. Brain In Play has designed this abbreviated BPE Youth Fast-Track with as many evidence-based fail-safes as possible given what is at stake for youth brains.

Finally, activators are necessary to engage and sustain healthcare behavior change for most individuals. In the case of youth sports, ac-tivators are especially important to help offset the powerful status-quo culture of sports, and to help players both gain a foothold with some or all BPE-Youth best practices and to achieve some consistency over time with new routines. We included the 'Honor Code' activation because it is emotional and honorable, as well being the 'black and white' right thing to do. It also adds the element of being part of a powerful and high-integrity 'group-think' that can *quickly* help youth athletes build support for change, locally and from around the world.

For parents and coaches, introducing a simple Code of Honor and Behavior that stops young athletes from playing head hurt and gets them started on simple targeted behaviors to improve brain health and resilience so brain injury prevention, healing and consequence-avoidance is optimized...*does* it *get* any better than that?

BPE Youth Fast-Track Details: BE CHAMPS 24/7

B: Breathing to Focus

Breathing to Focus involves a deep breathing relaxation response exercise that is recommended twice per day to power up and positively refresh and focus the brain on that which is most important in a person's life. It's almost like turning on a computer in the morning and seeing those familiar icons on the screen – that are really shortcuts to critical programs and online content. What if I told you that ten minutes in the morning when you wake up and ten minutes at night just before going to sleep is all it takes to begin to help make this same kind of powered-up relaxation response happen with that onboard computer in our heads called the brain? It's true (consisting of relaxed deep breathing, clearing your mind and then creating specific positive images of sports, academic, social and/or spiritual life success).

Considering the second ten minutes is just before sleep, it really only means ten minutes of *extra* effort a day, for which you will gain huge returns – not the least of which is to set the tone for a great day, one that is more relaxed and super-focused (so one actually gains back that ten minutes several fold each day with the efficiencies that come with being more focused and less distracted and anxious). Of course if you could find an extra ten minutes at mid-day, this will develop more technique competency and help your brain achieve a more consistent sense of relaxed wellbeing (as well as further increasing brain cell functioning and growth.).

The *Breathing to Focus* Relaxation Response

There are many techniques that produce what experts call the relaxation response, if you are already familiar with one that you are comfortable with consider reloading on that one. The key is to commit to doing the technique at least ten minutes twice per day, upon awakening in the morning and going to bed at night, and focusing on creating a positive image in your mind of your athletic or life success. One of the simplest and best forms of this is as follows:

Breathing to Focus Relaxation Response Technique

1. Find a quiet relaxing place to sit (same place always) ideally with your feet up (can be in bed with your back up straight and head supported by pillows);

2. Close your eyes.

3. Breathe in slowly through your nose to a count of 3, hold your breath for a count of 4 and exhale through your mouth blowing slowly through your lips for a count of 5. Become aware of your relaxed breathing;

4. Start to tighten and then relax your muscles a few seconds at a time, beginning with your toes and progressing up to your forehead. Keep all muscles relaxed and continue breathing;

5. As you get this going, picture in your mind a positive image of athletic or life success. Continue for ten minutes (or a bit longer if you can). You may open your eyes to check on time but don't use a timer or alarm. When you are finished sit quietly in transition for a few minutes;

6. If distracting thoughts come, push them from your mind and focus on that image of your athletic or life success.

So what exactly does this best practice also referred to as *mindfulness*, do for your brain? The impact of mindfulness includes reversing brain cell inflammation and oxidative stress, that after decades of neuroscience research, have been traced to specific gene pathways.[57] A recent study has confirmed that a consistent relaxation response produces ongoing changes in gene expression that improves immune function, energy metabolism and insulin secretion, while reducing cell inflammation – all of which maximize brain health.[58]

Finally, thanks to advanced imaging and analysis techniques, a breakthrough research study on mindfulness shows consistently practicing the relaxation response *produces gray matter brain cell density growth in brain regions involved with learning and memory processing (hippocampus), and emotional regulation (amygdala)*, among others, in *as quickly as six to eight weeks in college students newly trained in the relaxation response.*[59] Refer to this referenced study to view before and after images of these changed brain regions.

Bottom Line: To reduce the risks of and heal the damage from concussions and A-SCBs, as well as do prevention maintenance after concussion recovery, this first BPE Youth mindfulness best practice is a must. *The point that the brain regions specifically improved include two of the same regions that are selectively damaged by sports head injuries should not be lost on the Big-3 (hippocampus and amygdala).*

The relaxation response slowly but surely also lowers one's level of cortisol (the stress hormone). Cortisol reduction ensures that more brain cells will function at their best and facilitates new brain cell growth[60] (soon further discussed as a separate best practice). The advantages of being more relaxed and focused are linked to multiple life successes that the Big-3 does not need us to list here. However, in terms of sports head injury prevention there is no doubt that relaxed and focused athletes on the field will be much more prepared to make better instantaneous and calculated game related decisions and to better anticipate, and respond to concussive impacts, compared to a more stressed out, distracted and intense peers.

The reason for doing focused breathing upon awakening is to start each day with a preemptive positive and relaxed headset. The motive for doing the second brain focusing exercise at bedtime is that this helps facilitate falling asleep – and sleep is critically important to head injury prevention, brain cell wellness and growth (more on this later).

Before closing on this I want to mention the practice of Yoga as a potential adjunct or add-on to *Breathing To Focus*, with regard to facilitating similar relaxation response outcomes as those described in this chapter section. Many professional athletes are finding certain types of Yoga practice helpful to achieve focus and relaxation while simultaneously improving strength and flexibility. Most do not know that they are also improving brain cell wellness and growth.

E: Exercise

Exercise for many youth athletes is perhaps the easiest BPE Youth threshold to meet once 'BPE Youth activated'. The minimum requirement involves doing 45 consecutive minutes of light aerobic exercise three times per week or 30 minutes four times per week, which many athletes might already be achieving as part of their team participation in practices/games where continuous light running is the order of the day (soccer, football, hockey, lacrosse, basketball etc.). But should this not be so, there is no better way than **endurance exercise** to get many of the brain wellness good gene expressions we have talked about switched on, powered up and online.

Meeting this minimal standard isn't about hard core intense exercising or fast jogging runs, but instead is recommended to consist of light jogging or light aerobic work outs on a cross training machine. Fast power walking works also. This is because many hard-core athletes tend to work out too much which creates that oxidative build up we have talked about that our brain cells then have to divert more energy to dispose of, taking resources away from productive healthy cellular activities (like growing new cells). There is a growing baseline of neuroscience research supporting this *light but longer aerobic exercise* routine known as **endurance exercise** to enhance the functioning, preservation and growth of hippocampal brain cells and improve memory and cognition (complex thinking). In fact scientists in 2013 traced how exercise makes this happen all the way back to neuro-epigenetic gene activation[61] *(PGC-1α/FNDC5 gene pathway)*.

One of the first major endurance exercise research studies[62] was done on adults, comparing 2 groups: one group did 45 minutes of aerobic endurance exercise three times per week, and the other group stretched 3 times per week for 45 minutes. Brain cell volumes were measured before the study and a year later in the brain's memory and learning center known to most readers as the hippocampus (H). The Aerobic Endurance Exercise Group increased their H volumes an average of 2% compared to the stretching group who *lost* an average of 1.4% of H volume, not unexpected due to normal aging. Doing the math shows a 3.4% net gain from endurance exercise in perhaps the most important part of the brain for net cell growth to be occurring.

This same research group wondered if exercise-fitness had the same effect on younger brains so compared preteen groups of fit and unfit children, finding that fit children had larger H-Brain volumes (incredibly by 12%) compared to unfit peers, and significantly outperformed their unfit peers on cognitive test scores as well.[63] ***This is one big reason why we need to continue youth sports - in addition to the many favorable intangibles previously mentioned.***

So what exactly is the substance that endurance exercise produces in muscles that activates the expression of good genes so brain cell functioning and growth are enhanced, much like a fertilizer for the brain? It's called **BDNF**, or *brain derived neurotrophic factor*. BDNF is why we feel so good and think so much more clearly after exercise and why some top executives are conducting strategy meetings while fast walking on treadmills. BDNF is what showed up in much larger quantities in the brains of those exercising adults that had 3.4% H-Brain net growth. BDNF's great news is that besides growing new brain cells, it also has emerged as a significant player in helping those new cells to survive, while also building synapses and developing synaptic connections.[66] Synapses are those bridge structures that exist between brain cells supporting them to communicate with each other.

Regarding exercise and stress, if the stress hormone cortisol rises above a certain level brain cell growth is prevented. Exercise (BDNF) reduces cortisol levels. This was just confirmed by a 2013 study which for the first time linked physical activity in youth to cortisol levels.[64] Thus, there are direct 1:1 connections between endurance exercise, BDNF, stress management and new brain cell production, all related to cortisol (detailed later in this chapter). In fact a recent study on exercise and brain cell growth linked endurance exercise with increased gray matter hippocampal growth in 18-45 year olds.[65]

BDNF has also been found to reverse depression[73], and should be part of every youth athlete's workout routine, given the link between youth concussion and depression (especially if there is a history of concussion). And in related 2014 research just published, one group of scientists propose BDNF's effects are so dramatic that it is the single most important gene determining concussion recovery.[66]

Bottom Line: In closing, the major exercise take-away for players is to conduct a careful inventory of your consistent light aerobic endurance exercising, planning to have at least have 3-4 workouts per week lasting 30-45 minutes each, year round. The only cautionary note is to make sure not to overdo it, as too much aerobic exercise produces toxic oxidant buildup, which reduces rather than promotes brain health at cellular levels. To reiterate, we are talking about slow jogging, fast power walking or sessions on a cross-trainer.

C: Cortisol Reduction

Cortisol is the stress hormone, which in therapeutic amounts is healthy. However, when stress levels rise too high, so does cortisol and individuals begin to break down mentally and physically. Continuously elevated cortisol increases brain vulnerability for injuries and diseases, due to chronic cell inflammation and toxic oxidant buildup.[67]

The most important dynamic for BPE Youth Fast Track that bears repeating is that if **cortisol levels rise past a certain point or threshold, neurogenesis (brain cell growth) is prevented**. The shutoff mechanism for how and why this happens has only been recently discovered and predictably is the result of 'bad' gene expression.[68] Consistently lowering cortisol (stress) to therapeutic (manageable) levels greatly improves the functioning, preservation and growth of brain cells, causing the associated upsides of top brain performance and resilience, essential for prevention and healing of brain injuries.

The most basic way to keep cortisol in therapeutic check is to manage stress well. Starting (and ending) each day with *Breathing to Focus* is a step in the right direction, but this should be complemented by proactive efforts to specifically reduce what we call 'stress tolerations' or the triggers of our psychosocial stress. It might sound elementary, but taking the time to write down and prioritize a list of what is causing the most stress in our lives, and then identifying ways to remove these tolerations helps to reduce stress/cortisol. While it may be that some stress tolerations on 'the' list are out of one's control to be completely eliminated, it is likely most are within one's ower to be fully or partially resolved. There is even some stress relief that comes from making the list, as it makes more manageable that which can seem to be an overwhelming mass of nervous anxiety. The list can also serve as talking points so one can more easily process worries about stress with trusted others and get feedback or help for how to best manage it (further reducing stress and cortisol).

There are also some simple proven ways for to reduce stress, starting with planning to get a good night's sleep. Just one night of bad sleep often results in a 50% increase in circulating cortisol.[69] In other words, *not having* a consistent routine of sleeping a minimum of seven to eight hours a night significantly increases one's cortisol over time. Besides restful sleep, listed below are some simple cortisol reduction *short-term* strategies to use when stress increases, or to build in proactively for reliably better stress management on a more regular basis (and approximate percentages of cortisol/stress reduction):

➤ Listening to favorite music - 66%
➤ Spending time with funny best friend and laughing – 39%
➤ Doing something that has spiritual meaning for you – 25%
➤ Meditation/Yoga – 20% (consistent routine further increases)
➤ Drinking green or black tea – 47%
➤ Chewing favorite gum – 12-16%
➤ Getting a massage – 31%

Regarding brain functioning, the following athletic performance abilities are impaired by stress overload: concentration decision-making, problem solving, emotional stability, memory, learning, and recognition awareness. So the Big-3 as a group should prioritize cortisol reduction, as it is a BPE-Youth best-practice that is *all upside* in support of youth brain development and wellness, from academic success to mental health, athletic prowess and injury avoidance.

Bottom Line: Start each day with renewed commitment to breathing to focus, take action on your tolerations list by ticking off one or a few minor ones every day or so, or take action on one big priority stress toleration, being careful to not take on too much at once. Then assure improved stress management by adding in some of those cortisol reducers, avoiding high-stress people, places and things, and consistently get a good night's sleep (more on sleep coming up).

H: Honor Code

Brain In Play International's BPE Youth Fast-Track supports youth athletes to adhere to a bottom line Code of Honor and Behavior that locks players into conduct that improves brain health for themselves and teammates. This begins for athletes with the 'Code' mandate that no player shall ever play head hurt under any circumstances, starting of course with themselves. After getting this far in the book, athletes, parents and coaches have been exposed to irrefutable evidence for why this is necessary, backed up by the latest research and targeted case examples, one fatally catastrophic in the case of 17-year-old football star Nathan Stiles. After speaking with Nathan's father Ron Stiles, there is no better way to honor this young man and celebrate his life by committing to the Honor Code (doing the right thing) and spreading the word about it, so second impact syndrome is eliminated.

The Code serves as both a cultural catalyst supporting player brain health and as activator to sustain BPE Youth best practices long-term. It is sometimes hard to step up and lead needed change by example, even when something is the right thing to do. But we are hoping this call to Honor the Code will be easier for all Big-3 now that you are part of an inner circle that fully understands that brains and lives really are on the line-every day across the globe. In fact we are hoping that this new knowledge serves to emotionally engage and sustain players as they take on BPE Youth for their own sports head injury prevention, healing and consequence avoidance purposes. And knowing there is honor in adhering to The Code, especially doing it on behalf of others like teammates and coaches, it is definitely activating.

The Code philosophy is consistent with a zero tolerance approach for preventable sports head injuries and aligns with the latest neuroscience research which shows head injuries are cumulative. This means head-hurt players suffering additional head injuries are candidates for more severe and potentially catastrophic brain damage. The reader may recall that concussed players are three times more likely to suffer additional concussions. This means that unaddressed, the brain's threshold for subsequent concussions is always lowering, unless there is a BPE Youth commitment to turn this vulnerability around by engaging in behaviors that decrease chronic inflammation and oxidative stress, and grow brain cells.

BPE Youth's Code is described in detail next chapter and recommended as a way to structure up a youth athlete's commitment to his/her best brain health, along with the injury avoidance, and athletic/academic performance enhancement that comes along with it.

A: Auto-regulation
Sleep, Hydration & Muscle Condition (Neck Strength)

Introduction: Auto-regulation consists of three biological processes that must be part of a youth athlete's everyday life so the brain-body health connection is maximized. It involves consistently building in the right amount of sleep, hydration and muscle conditioning (focus on neck strength) so that athletes develop a baseline or threshold of brain and body health that helps prevent or minimize injuries. If you think about youth athletes being like *race cars*, auto-regulation begins to make more sense. A race car driver would never let his/her car run low on oil (sleep), demanding the best grade and keeping it full/level. The same is true for gas (hydration) and maintaining the rest of the car in top condition (think muscles). While I am not a NASCAR expert, I do know about races being won or lost because race-teams didn't anticipate these three auto-regulation analogs well enough in advance.

Racing cars, not unlike youth brains/bodies, are complicated machines that require continuous fine tuning to consistently perform at a highest levels and to avoid crashes especially at high risk turns, that if poorly negotiated will usually end their ability to compete. Modern sports has certainly recognized this comparison, jump started by Michael Jordan who back in the 1980s kick-started year-round muscle conditioning and nutritional training up to another gear (and proceeded to win three additional NBA championships while staying injury free after leaving the rigorous sport of basketball for a couple of years to play much more sedentary baseball). This same auto-regulation conditioning applies to youth contact sports, especially with regard to toning and strengthening the brain's shock-absorbing neck muscles which help limit the head's rag doll effect that results from unanticipated concussive head and body slam impacts (and associated linear back and forth, and side-ways twisting rotations of the brain). In addition, given what we now know about the mega value of BDNF related to brain wellness, close attention must be paid to the injury prevention of muscles needed for routine endurance exercise training.

Sleep:

The brain health benefits of getting good sleep are so numerous they could fill the pages of an entire book. We already mentioned the connection between lack of sleep and excess cortisol, which causes brain cell dysfunction and prevents the growth of neurons. The day-to-day impact of not getting enough sleep is that youth athletes 'sleep-walk' around, much less athletically, academically and emotionally sharp than they normally would be. And the connection between being less brain sharp leading to more head injuries on the field/court/rink is an obvious one. Adding chronic sleep deprivation or sleepiness to the equation increases the risk of injury up to ten fold. Here are other key brain health reasons for getting 7-8 hours of sleep:

1. BDNF: In October 2013 for the first time lack of sleep was officially linked to both increased stress (cortisol) and reduced BDNF levels (the brain's fertilizer);[70]
2. Disease/Injury vulnerability: A 2013 youth study confirmed lack of sleep causes increased chronic cell inflammation, organ vulnerability (to disease and injury), and leads to many chronic inflammatory conditions including shutting down of the immune system, and obesity;[76]
3. Psychomotor performance and pro-inflammation: A research study on young men and women found modest sleep loss associated with major daytime sleepiness, impaired psychomotor performance (muscle coordination/movement) and release of pro-inflammatory cytokines[67] which leads to chronic inflammation of brain cells, none of which is good for athletes!

Sleep Bottom Line:

A bedtime routine is critical for any serious athlete, which means going to bed the same time every night (or close to it) and developing a consistent before sleep ritual. The athlete needs to limit ingesting any beverage or food that contains caffeine after 3pm to avoid having trouble falling asleep (for some it might have to be noon). These are foods and drinks such as coffee, sodas or dark chocolates (check food labels). Avoid large meals or high-sugar snacks close to bedtime (shouldn't be eating in this manner anyway). Also know that drinking alcoholic beverages or using marijuana prevents deepest REM sleep from happening (which is the highest quality most restorative sleep – more on this later). Some common sense bedtime basics also must prevail, including refraining from stimulating activities or TV shows in the hour just before sleep and no heavy exercise during evening hours, which can also prevent falling asleep. Also computers/IPADs must be turned off a few hours before bed, as these blue screens extract some of our melatonin, which helps to keep us awake.

It is recommended that everyone take a step back and evaluate their physical sleeping quarters and situations, looking for ways to ensure a more quiet and restful sleep (including moving pets to the floor or being sectioned off if their 'comings and goings' disrupt sleep). If your bedroom is such that at first light it gets very bright, add window shades or wear eye shades while sleeping. Lastly, once in bed consider BPE Youth's *Breathing to Focus* relaxation response which works like a cross between the old-school combination of a warm glass of milk and counting sheep, setting your brain cells up for restful sleep and accelerated growth.

Hydration:

Dr. Ashare has been a longtime proponent of eight full glasses of water per day as a baseline of youth sports hydration, and adding more water or healthy replacement drinks in advance of and during hard practices and games, especially on hotter days outside or warmer indoor situations. In his 25 years on the bench as a team doctor caring for elite world class youth hockey stars he has observed those that hydrate this way have much better third periods. When asked what this means Doc will tell you convincingly, "More goals and less injuries for sure!" His USA Junior Hockey Teams' international success over the years is anecdotal proof enough. And most heard about what happened with Lebron James during the fourth quarter of the NBA finals in sweltering San Antonio when his hydration prep failed him. During the first game of the finals that his team was convincingly winning in the fourth quarter, dehydration got him benched, writhing in pain and unable to reenter the game, resulting in a huge loss for his team – and likely costing them a championship.

However, the main issue with head injuries and adequate fluids is that even mild dehydration begins to shrink the adolescent brain.[78] As dehydration evolves, a larger gap gets created between the soft brain and the hard skull (the subarachnoid space). This causes more potential for concussion and increased severity of axon (communication cell) damage, because the brain has more area to move back and forth and rotate in, crashing and twisting against the skull at higher acceleration and deceleration speeds because of this larger space.

This shock absorbing protective property of hydration to reduce the severity of sports brain injury has gone largely underestimated by most clinician scientists, but not Dr. Ashare, a biomechanical-physics expert who in May 2014 edited the leading technical book on the mechanism of concussion in sports. 'Doc' had us create and show a model of brain dehydration (shrinkage) before an auditorium of full of sports coaches. Even we were surprised by the increased damage just an extra quarter or half inch of space causes to a soft mass when it accelerates and decelerates (starts and stops) very quickly in a confined space with hard walls. And we only modeled linear (straight back and forth) start-stops. Coaches walked away also thinking about even the A-SCBs implications of dehydration. Imagine in one season of practices and games how more damaging those accumulated hundreds of mini starts and stops would be if the brain was able to move around inside the skull just a bit more...and this is preventable.

The bottom lines:
1. Establish your hydration baseline well in advance and increase your fluid intake in prep for games and practices. Remember, not even Lebron James can catch up on hydration.
2. Diet sodas and other caffeine containing fluids are not to be included in routine hydration prep, as they actually cause dehydration because caffeine acts as a diuretic, causing increased urination and fluid loss.
3. Best tip on what to include as part of your pre/during game hydration: Green Tea from extract that is unsweetened, suggest Honest Brand Tea (as Green Tea from extract also helps improves short term cognition significantly).[77]

General Muscle and Neck Strength Conditioning:

There are several ways that help keep muscles in great condition both in and out of season. A slow consistent 30-45 minute jog 3-5 times per week while holding 1-2lb weights can be a great way to maintain strength and tone while driving and maintaining your BDNF production. Again, such a regimen should not be added to an in-season practice/game schedule if it results in being overtired or overextended in any way. The point is to drive BDNF production and keep muscles optimally conditioned, not risk musculoskeletal or head injuries from overuse and buildup of toxic oxidants.

New ways are emerging to help keep muscles from getting injured and to help more continuously refresh them after major exertion, from therapeutic massage to Muscle Activation Therapy or MAT which our NFL clients and many world-class endurance exercisers utilize regularly (a well-kept secret is the Denver Broncos have a full time MAT consultant). Depending on how intense your sport is, or how high-risk its practices and games might be for overuse injuries, you may consider one of these integrative therapies. The ideal scenario is to recover quickly from intense strength workouts or game-days to be able to adhere to your endurance exercise routine and produce that BDNF.

Muscle/Neck Strength Therapies:

In the case of neck strengthening, there is enough evidence to suggest this is no longer an elective option, but is a must have for youth players of both genders seeking to avoid sports head injury. A great comprehensive and easy to follow protocol is offered by Strength & Conditioning Coach Joe Giandonato MS, CSCS. His list of nine excellent neck strengthening exercises take only minutes and you can work them into formal workouts three to four times per week and select a few that you can do while stopped at a red light, walking to your next class or waiting in line. Coach Giandonato's regimen can be found at: (http://performancecenter.stack.com/article_detail.jsp?id=63125#wall Default)

M: Meals Change Brains:

This will be a quick and simple brain health diet primer focused on priority nutritional tips that optimize brain cell functioning, preservation and growth. It is purposely basic and includes general tips on what to eat to keep brain cells happy, and what not to eat to avoid chronic inflammation and toxic oxidant(s) build up. And should you want more detailed brain nutrition info, you will learn where to go.

I will be sharing what has successfully helped our young Pro-Athlete clientele (one who returned saying "I had the best nutritional experts on my 3 NFL Teams and I was never able to understand the basics so my post-concussion symptoms never got better until now, and my performance work-outs are better."). Keeping things simple is best when it comes to changing nutrition, whether one is an athlete or a food scientist. The important take away is that foods have a quick and in some cases immediate impact on upgrading or downgrading brain cell functioning, preservation and growth (in addition to having longer term good or bad brain/body health consequences).

Before closing this *Meals Change Brains* introduction, let's not omit the brain-food issue that often gets overlooked, despite impacting 30% of the population. Three out of every ten Americans has gluten sensitivity, essentially making gluten a neurotoxin. Thanks to the American Academy of Neurology's Dr. David Perlmutter, more light is being shed on gluten.[75] Even if you are not one of these unlucky 30%, a gluten-free or restricted, low carb diet that excludes refined sugars and bad fats, and adds good omega-3 fats and colorful vegetables, among the best nutrition for top brain health.

Let's start with foods to stay away from that make most athletes who avoid them feel brain-sharper within hours or days, and lift that brain fog of post-concussive syndrome fairly quickly (our clinical experience with adolescents and adults). Then get to the good foods.

Foods Bad for the Brain (causes toxic oxidant build-up):

Eliminate: sugary foods (any with added or refined sugar), fast-foods, foods colored white (white bread, pastas), and foods that are canned, boxed, fried or processed (no cold cuts); limit red meats to lean portions once/twice per week and avoid beverages that are sweetened, alcoholic and sodas, including regular and diet. Eliminate unhealthy high fat and salty foods and do not add salt to your food.

Brain Smart Foods (most of which are anti-oxidants):

Do eat fresh fruits (blueberries, red grapes), salads, greens (especially kale), colorful vegetables, nuts (walnuts), fresh fish (wild salmon, shrimp, lobster), eggs, yogurts, high fiber-foods, organically raised poultry and beef. Healthy fats (omega-3s), low carbohydrates and moderate amounts of protein are suggested. Virgin olive oil is good and use of pepper is fine. Choose organic when possible, as the pesticides used to enhance fruits/vegetables are neurotoxic. Carbohydrate food content can be checked at www.ndb.nal.usda.gov

Brain Smart Beverages:

Drink lots of green tea from green tea extract, water, and occasional cups of coffee before 3pm (a more potent antioxidant than we ever realized). Green tea extract enhances connectivity between the brain's parietal (side) and frontal lobes during memory processing suggesting positive short-term neuroplasticity changes greatly improving cognition.[77] Thus, mixing **green tea extract** combined with your beverage of choice is suggested for pregame and game-time hydration.

Other Food Tips:

Beware of whole grains that have a sneaky high glycemic index (this means they raise the blood sugar too high too quickly). Whole grain bread marketed as great for you is preferable to white bread, but Ezekial bread from the frozen food section is best for toast in the morning. And speaking of the morning, never skip breakfast.

If you want to do the absolute very best for your brain health from a nutritional standpoint, Google Dr. David Perlmutter's Brain-Change website at www.DrPerlmutter.com. There you will find all that you need to know about both glycemic index (how to keep one's blood sugar from rising fast to keep it healthily stable which is best for brains) and gluten (what is now being identified as bad for the brain and a cause for Alzheimer's). While the research on gluten is still considered controversial by some, our anecdotal patient reports of feeling better and more brain sharp after restricting or stopping gluten are too impressive to ignore. Dr. Perlmutter's site includes genomic food research papers and a shopping list for mom/dad with the best foods to buy for brain health. And surprisingly, a recent study showed that if one is judicious, it doesn't cost more to eat a totally brain-healthy diet, versus one that leads to brain cell inflammation and oxidative stress.

P: Plan & Track:

A major activator that truly helps engage and sustain healthy lifestyle change is having a formal plan to follow and then to track it daily or several times per week (i.e., this can be as simple as listing those BPE Youth Fast-Track behaviors you are committed to on your smart phone notes page and check-listing your progress daily). There are a many Activity Smart-Apps which track various activities such as diet, weight, activity level, fitness and sleep, with reminder schedules that can be programmed, one of which is free called *My Fitness Pal* (www.MyFitnessPal.com). For high tech wristband wearing youth athletes who have part time jobs or birthdays coming up, there are some accessory bracelets that track activity level, steps and sleep. The NY Times runs an ongoing review section comparing activity trackers from the $100 Fit-Bit to the $149 Nike Fuelband SE (Google NY Times Activity Trackers). And then there is the old-school journaling method where you write out your three to six BPE Youth practices you are tracking in a handwritten journal kept at your bedside or desk. Using a tracking method is a key activator that really does help jump-start and sustain follow-up with desired lifestyle changes, and is highly suggested for BPE Youth's brain saving BE CHAMPS – 24/7.

S: Substance Use

The S in CHAMPS is for recreational or binge use of 'Substances' that cause brain damage from that now familiar dual common denom-inator of chronic inflammation and toxic oxidant build-up, as well as from direct brain cell fatal exposure to these substances.

We are referring primarily to using alcohol and marijuana, both of which have just been found (2013/2014) to be much more neurotoxic (bad for the brain) than scientists imagined – as both in small amounts impair brain functioning AND damage brain structure. In this case, 'best-practice' is avoiding/abstaining from using alcohol or marijuana.

Let's review alcohol first. A 2013 analysis of the top research involving alcohol and youth brains entitled, *Pathways to Alcohol-Induced Brain Impairment in Young People: A Review* was published in the esteemed brain health medical journal Cortex.[79] The study's bottom line: Having more than three to four drinks for young women and more than five for young men at any one sitting produces white matter brain damage. If this were to become a routine, sophisticated imaging shows that shrinking of the brain and significant damage to white matter tracts or pathways will result. This clinically means impaired visual learning, memory, decision making and critical thinking – not a good thing if you are an athlete, especially if wanting to be at your best, to avoid injury, athletically excel, stay academically eligible or get to that next level. We are told by the study's authors that those brain functions most impaired by alcohol are located in the hippocampus and frontal structures of the brain – which we know are not fully mature until 24 or 25 years of age. Let's recall the hippocampus is selectively injured by repetitive head trauma – so we are talking a potential "double-whammy" of brain damage here.

And speaking of the hippocampus, another new study found moderate use of alcohol significantly decreases neurogenesis (brain cell growth) in adults – again, not a state of affairs any youth athlete wants happening in the hippocampal region of their brains.[80] A study recently done with 18-25 year old week-end binge drinkers found the same four drinks for women and five drinks limit for men on single occasions was all it took to find evidence for thinning of the brain's prefrontal cortex--where important thinking, decision making, paying attention, planning and processing emotions takes place.[79]

To close on alcohol, a *June 2014 Bio-Science Journal* article that youth athletes should know about entitled, **Single Episode of Binge Drinking Linked to Gut Leakage and Immune System Effects**, informs one night of drinking causes leakage of bacterial endotoxins from the intestines into the blood stream, causing inflammation, tissue damage and major immune system dysfunction. [81]

On the marijuana front things are just as concerning, if not more surprising. Incredibly not more than a few months after some U.S. states legalized marijuana for sale on the assumption that casual use was not harmful, an April 2014 study from Northwestern Medicine, Massachusetts General Hospital and Harvard Medical School has determined otherwise.[82] Findings show that casual use (smoking 1-2 times per week) changes the brain's structure in two regions involved with motivation and emotional control in 18-25 year old college students. One of these gray matter areas is the amygdala, selectively damaged in repetitive sports head trauma and implicated as a cause of depression in those with concussions – again, the clinically dangerous 'double-whammy' phenomenon. In other words, the brain damage this drug causes to the amygdala adds to the already existing brain trauma of concussion/A-SCBs, further ravaging this grey matter brain part. And in June 2014 the prestigious New England Journal of Medicine released a summary of marijuana's negative health effects focused on teenage brains. It showcased that deficits in critical thinking and memory persist for days after marihuana use, with habitual teen use associated with lowered IQ that extends into adulthood.[83]

As a former faculty member of Brown University's Center for Alcohol & other Addictions Studies who taught alcohol/drug addiction at Brown Medical School to triple board resident physicians, it is helpful to no longer be guessing about whether serious damage is caused by these two recreational drugs that youth (and adults) most commonly use in America. Further, it helps to know that for both drugs, the quantity needed for brain damage is fairly small - an amount that most high school and college athletes (and adults) would consider casual.

To close on this youth best-practice, it is important to mention two things. First, to remind athletes about the overlap between use of these drugs and the negative impact on the best-practice of sleep (and with impaired sleep brings less REM brain restorative rest and increased cortisol, meaning no new brain cell growth etc.). Second is the potential for addiction, as both drugs require increasing brain damaging amounts over time to achieve the same psychoactive effect.

Bottom Line:

BPE-Youth recommends total abstinence from using alcohol and marijuana, given these substances are now known to cause brain damage even in small amounts. Such a recommendation is consistent with improving the functioning, preservation and growth of brain cells - as both of these drugs do exactly the opposite and will just make the damage from A-SCBs and concussion even worse. This likely aligns with most school codes of behavior anyway for student athletes that typically enforce a zero-tolerance policy regarding use of alcohol, marijuana and other psychoactive recreational drugs.

BPE Youth Fast-Track: BE CHAMPS - 24/7 Conclusion

In closing this major chapter, we must remind all readers that the BPE Youth Fast-Track's primary use is to reduce the risk for sports head injuries. Thus, this program best serves healthy youth athletes, particularly those seeking to avoid a first concussion, and especially previously concussed healthy youth desiring a best strategy to prevent subsequent concussion(s) and offset A-SCBs effects. Additionally BPE Youth's best practices help optimize brain wellness in those recovering from concussions/A-SCBs symptoms. In all scenarios above, players must notify parents of their intent to pursue some or all of BPE Youth Fast-Track so that family physicians are informed for their approval. It is never permissible for youth, parents or coaches to use BPE Fast-Track as a concussion recovery intervention without the supervision of an MD or Licensed Independent Practitioner (board certified psychologist or nurse practitioner/clinical specialist).

Finally, regarding BPE Youth Fast Track's 'six' best practices, we prefer youth athletes to consider them because it is what they choose to do, given it is best for their brain health, athletic performance and academic execution. Speaking of what is truly a brain safety best practice that extends to influencing the culture of youth sports, it is time to drill down further on BPE Youth's Code of Honor and Behavior.

Post Script August 19, 2014: The same research group that found aerobically fit pre-teens have increased gray brain cell matter and higher cognitive test scores compared to unfit peers, has just discovered that exercise/aerobic fitness also increases the fibrousness and compactness of the brain's white matter in nine and ten year olds (a major find and one more reason for why youth sports must continue).

CHAPTER TWELVE

BPE Youth Fast-Track Honor Code
'No Big-3 Leaves Any Player In Danger or Behind'

"The two most important days in your life are the day you are born, and the day you find out why" ~ Mark Twain

One of the most exciting parts of BPE-Youth Fast Track is its Honor Code (the H in BE CHAMPS-24/7). Simply put it helps prevent youth athletes from playing head hurt, the most important first priority in all of youth sports today. It can also help activate youth players and the rest of the Big-3 to be more fully supportive of BPE-Youth's six brain wellness best practices, *an athlete's fast-track to improved brain cell functioning, preservation and growth.*

Codes of Honor and Behavior are established for very important causes to standardize a priority set of beliefs and ways of behaving for communities, groups, or teams committed to the cause, consistent with the core values of the cause being honored. In the case of the youth sports brain injuries cause, it is best if we break down these words into simpler terms: youth, sports, and brain injuries. This will make it clear just how critical this issue is to the Big-3 and all those who care about youth and have loved ones playing youth contact sports.

For youth who continue to play organized competitive sports from middle school into high school or college, sports is likely at the center of their lives. For parents, other than spouses or life partners, there is no one more important that even comes close to their beloved children (a.k.a. youth) For coaches, there is no question that coaching youth sports is a labor of love and a huge part of their lives.

What this leaves us with is the term brain injuries caused by youth sports, which is the most concerning issue that all Big-3 share in common and will soon gain a higher public profile, given the White House Summit, The Institute of Medicine's concussion investigation (as more individuals actually hear about and read the IOM Report), and as more parents learn about the testimony of experts that traumatic brain injury (90% are concussions) already is a leading cause of long-term disability under age forty-five in the U.S.. It's only a matter of time before the media gets a handle on what's really going on with these latest DTI studies showing significant hippocampal brain damage and shrinkage in college athletes—from only subconcussive impacts; damage that these studies show is worsened by a having history of concussion. This discovery, on top of learning that many post-concussed youth athletes are likely being returned back to sports and classrooms before they are fully healed, will not go over well with many parents.

Thus, the cause for an Honor Code seems most convincing: that developing brains in our middle-high school and college athletes need protection from sports-related traumatic head injury that could render them brain damaged. So what might be the problem with, or barriers to, achieving immediate 100% support from all stakeholders?

➢ A powerful, longstanding sports culture code that says "suck it up", "gut it out" and play on;

➢ A culture where if you take time off, it's acceptable to be replaced in a heartbeat and lose your starting position;

- A sports culture code that says prioritizing an intangible injury means you are "weak";
- A culture that says the team is more important than the individual and sacrifices like playing hurt are necessary;
- A sports culture code that only recently acknowledged that getting your bell rung was an injury worth mentioning;
- A culture code that respects being able to take a hit and get right back up – "The Gladiator" mentality;
- A sports culture glorifying big hits, crashes and tough play (leading the highlight shows on ESPN and NHL Tonight) ;
- A sports culture code that most athletes have been groomed around since birth.

So what is changing that will stop us in our tracks and consider *adjusting* this culture of youth sports *to reduce* head injuries?

What is definitely changing is that the public is slowly coming to understand and accept that concussive head injuries do cause serious brain harm that lasts longer than previously realized. This awareness comes in part from watching *"60 Minutes"* about lasting military and football concussion damage, and learning of pro and college football players quitting early to avoid permanent brain damage because they already are impaired, and still others seriously injured in their prime who couldn't return to play even if they wanted to. And then there are the high profile youth sports deaths from second impact syndrome that just keep on coming, the latest being Will McKamey, a 19 year old Naval Academy football player who died of second impact syndrome on March 27, 2014 at the University of Maryland Shock Trauma Center in Baltimore – the very same medical center where college fullback Derek Sheely previously died of this same concussive/ACBs consequence. The tipping point for change may be a growing awareness about early stage CTE being diagnosed in teenagers (a disease resulting in early dementia). As a result, in a year or two, the following subjects are likely soon to be standard water-cooler talk:

-SCBs that accumulate cause DTI brain damage similar to concussion
-White matter brain damage in men's and women's college hockey
-Hippocampal shrinkage in college football players absent concussion
-Concussions/A-SCBs damage is cumulative (damage just adds up)
-Soccer is dangerous also, causing white and grey matter damage
-HS/College women have most concussions per hours played
-Catastrophic outcomes do happen: second impact syndrome/paralysis
-Sports brain damage can cause chronic depression and suicides
-Playing head hurt is single most high-risk brain damaging activity.
-Brains compromised by previous injuries will experience greater damage from the next hit and are more vulnerable than others to experience a persistent post-concussion syndrome lasting months to years, potentially fatal second impact syndrome, and/or depression.
-Most players hide symptoms, youth-pros, worsening all the above.

Thus, the context for an immediate youth sports culture change grounded in a Code of Honor and Behavior that manages youth sports head injuries and their potential catastrophic outcomes with a zero tolerance policy for playing head hurt, seems as justified as it could possibly be. Those who know about these newly confirmed DTI brain damage realities must aggressively lead the way—with players, parents and coaches out front on this one!

Culture Change Next Steps

It's time now for a sea change, a marked transformation that is so incredibly powerful it can't be stopped and will dictate just how things will be going forward. Just think of Mother Nature and a rogue wave, because that's what this chapter recommends the Big-3 consider. In the rogue wave's wake youth athletes and their brains are truly prioritized, parents can breathe easier and with more confidence, and great youth coaches won't back away from coaching because of worries about law suits, legitimized by a lack of appropriate culture standards and a nonexistent head injury code of conduct.

The Big-3 can't afford to wait for the convening of more blue ribbon concussion committees or additional White House or Institute of Medicine/CDC calls for action—there is no time to waste. In the instance of a worst-case head injury scenario that could have been prevented, one more is too many—whether it results in second impact syndrome, head/neck paralysis from a catastrophic collision, or a years-long persistent post-concussive syndrome. The brains and lives of our sons, daughters, siblings and grandchildren are too precious to gamble with, and deserve our committed leadership and support to turn this issue around immediately. Youth must be actively involved in making this "sea change" and Code of Honor and Behavior happen, whether playing hockey in Canada, football in the United States, soccer in Europe or Brazil, or rugby in Australia.

Step one in culture change will be taken if there is an overwhelming need for change. This criterion has been met—youth sports brain injuries in their current state of being, qualifies for a Code of Honor and Behavior to change its culture as quickly as possible. The Code must be one that the Big-3 will embrace, implement, and improve over time. The Code should be primarily lead by players themselves— supported strongly by loving parents and coaches who prioritize young players and their developing brains. The Code should keep it simple, while addressing the cultural norms and realities of both "youth sports" and brain injury and health. The Code must powerfully change how the Big-3 thinks and behaves about youth sports and related brain injury and health, so that the rest of the world organizes around it in response. The Code should serve clear notice, but be flexible enough so that it can be done one player, parent, and coach threesome at a time. For this is the only way we can make "overnight delivery" progress on this most critical issue of concern for youth athletes. They deserve more than our love—they deserve support, leadership, empowerment, and trust—so in a saying made famous a few generations ago at a once obscure racetrack in a place called Indianapolis: "Big-3, start your engines!"

[5] The U.S. Army's Football Team is all about "Honor"

BPE-Youth Fast-Track's Code of Honor/Behavior
[Which should be printed out and signed by all]

➤ All: I embrace the youth sports head injury Code of Honor's core values.*

➤ All: As a member of this team, I will be forthright, truthful, and honest at all times.

➤ Players: I will not play head-hurt under any conditions.

➤ Players: I will let my coach know when I have any symptoms of a head injury.

➤ Players: I will report to my head coach if I have knowledge of any players on my team that are playing or intend to play head-hurt.

➤ Captains/Players: I will strongly consider BPE Youth's best brain wellness practices as part of my athletic commitment.

> Captains: I will be a model of never playing head hurt and reporting those that do to the head coach.

> Coaching assistants: I will maintain the strict confidentiality of players reporting concerns about head hurt teammates and immediately tell shared information to the head coach.

> Parents: I agree to report to the head coach when my child has head-hurt symptoms.

> Head coach: I will take all reports of head-hurt players seriously and investigate.

> Head Coach: I will never knowingly play a head-hurt player under any conditions.

> Head Coach: Upon discovering any player having head injury symptoms, that player is immediately removed from that practice or game and his/her parents will be notified ASAP. An MD note will be required for return to team.

> **All: I will never leave a head hurt youth athlete in danger or behind**

VALUES: Brain health is top priority; honesty in all that we do; never leave a head hurt teammate behind to play in a practice or game.

The Code of Honor/Behavior is best introduced at an up-front mandatory meeting attended by all players, coaches and at least one parent. A short introduction acknowledging the serious problem of sports head injuries, mentioning the stat about the majority of head hurt players hiding concussion symptoms sets the reality-stage nicely. Sincerely conveying that the head coach believes it takes much more courage/guts to sit when head hurt, than it does to be tough enough to play helps change the culture. Educating players and parents that the most dangerous thing a player can do is play while head hurt due to the potential for catastrophic injury, is all it will take to orchestrate a unanimous signing-on of players and parents. Asking for their help and support and giving thanks for such in advance closes the deal.

Having been youth coaches, behavioral/brain health providers/LIPs or team physicians and league administrators for decades, we know that such a Code of Honor and behavior will be controversial at first, especially for certain teams and leagues. However, most coaches and league/school administrators will come around to understand the necessity for The Code given this issue is as serious as it gets, and after all, youth sports should be all about what's best for the kids. It's not if, but when the question will be asked of coaches and school/league administrators: "Were there things you could have done as a/the responsible adult to reduce the risk for youth head injuries that you failed to do?" And the individuals asking will not accept the reality of the youth sports culture as an excuse for not doing the right thing(s) given youth brains and lives are at stake.

Most coaches and administrators know if you have few rules that you are solid around, you will more likely get full cooperation and 100% player adherence. That is why the Code is simple and straightforward. We must remember that the most challenging and ominous thing about the latest head injury research is that more damage is happening to youth brains than we realized. And now that these insidious A-SCBs are part of the head injury equation, for any player with a concussion history one must always err on the side of caution to prevent the potential for a catastrophic outcome. The smartest decision a coach can make is to implement BPE Youth's head injury Code of Honor/Behavior and empower their team captains and coaching staffs to help consistently maintain it.

The next two chapters remind us why BPE Youth is so important and why we need to prioritize the prevention and best management of sports head injuries above all other things in youth sports. Chapter 13 delves into the issue of long term consequences from youth sports concussions and A-SCBs, and Chapter 14 illustrates how two committed innovators born a generation apart collaborated to make a difference to reduce catastrophic head injuries in youth.

CHAPTER THIRTEEN

Youth Sports Head Injury's Long-Term Consequences: To Worry or Not to Worry

There is only one-way to avoid criticism: do nothing,
say nothing and be nothing – Aristotle

This chapter is not intended to scare/worry members of the Big-3, but to address the reality of severe long-term consequences from re-petitive sports head injury. We also don't want the Big-3 to be blindsided by an excess volume of neuroscience research soon to flood the mainstream media linking repetitive head injuries with chronic traumatic encephalopathy (CTE) and Alzheimer's disease. This tsunami is already emerging in the clinician-scientist world. Most major media will soon run news features on this subject. The first wave will be set off by the C4CT Concussion Summit at the United Nations July 31, 2014, *which exclusively focuses on this issue.*

A Primer on Youth Sports Head Injury Long-term Consequences

One of the biggest fears of contact sports athletes, from college to the pro ranks (and their families) is getting long-term brain damage from concussions/A-SCBs. While in our research infancy regarding this, it is safe to say such fears are becoming increasingly legitimized.

This is because diseases such as CTE, Alzheimer's, and chronic major depression (some experts also include Parkinsonism and ALS) have recently all been implicated as directly or indirectly caused by repetitive head trauma. These illnesses have in common a neuro-inflammatory quality—meaning the brain's cells respond to recurring physical trauma by becoming chronically inflamed, which leads to less functional cells and the resulting buildup of what are called toxic oxidants (waste products from cell metabolism). The rule of thumb for any group of cells is that some acute inflammation is healthy and leads to healing, but chronic inflammation going unchecked is dangerously unhealthy and leads to increased disease and injury vulnerability. When repetitive head injury drives extreme levels of chronic inflammation and oxidative stress in that group of cells called *the brain*, the chance of developing CTE, chronic depression or Alzheimer's surges.

In the cases of CTE and Alzheimer's, chronic inflammation facilitates deposits of what are called tau proteins in the brain, destroying cells over time in specifically different ways depending on the disease. While CTE and Alzheimer's are separate diseases differentiated by their unique cell pathologies (on autopsy) and symptom patterns, both ultimately cause early dementia. Patients suffer severe memory loss and in final stages require 24/7 supervision. With head injury related chronic depression, this is also caused by trauma-induced chronic inflammation to select parts of the brain governing mood stabilization and emotions (particularly the brain's hippocampus and amygdala).

Many experts thought those first neuroscientists who cautioned the sports world at large about these longer-term consequences were overstating the cause for concern, since the earliest cases cited were high-profile football, hockey, and boxing pro athletes. They were challenging whether concussed high school/college athletes could realistically get CTE, since with boxers and NFL/NHL pros, there are years of hard-core game and practice head/body trauma.

In this regard you will recall that neuropathologist Dr. Ann McKee (BU/Bedford VA Brain Lab) recently confirmed 2 cases of CTE in the brains of teenage high school athletes, including Eric Pelly, the 18 year old son of Brain In Play advisor Joan Pelly, and Nathan Stiles whose story was told in Chapter 8. The reality of CTE in high school teenagers is a wakeup call for all of us. Indeed, Dr. McKee worries this could happen to anyone who is playing a high-risk contact sport who endures concussions or is overexposed to A-SCBs (please read: this does not say "everyone"—an important distinction, as Dr. McKee's opinion in this regard has been misinterpreted in the past).

Recently all three of this book's authors had the privilege of joining Dr. McKee at her VA/Boston Brain Lab where we observed her autopsy the brains of two pro athletes, while she taught us about CTE. Just before these autopsies we toured other parts of the brain lab and, under the microscope, observed the pathologically distinct brain damage that is CTE (in the same lab where, to date, all but one pro sports player brain autopsied exhibited CTE). The experience was transformational, as Dr. McKee poignantly described how brains diagnosed with late stage CTE were much smaller than normal and showed us the many cardinal signs that their brains had been ravaged by this illness. It is one thing to talk about CTE and quite another to observe it and see how this disease progresses over time in 4 stages to destroy what had once been beautiful brains.

The Net Translation:

In terms of how likely it is for youth athletes to be candidates for these serious repetitive head trauma disease consequences, the safest and honest answer is really *the same as it would be for any disease.* This means it depends on a blend of 2 factors, how genetically vulnerable is the athlete to get CTE, Alzheimer's, major depression, etcetera, and how much exposure the athlete has to concussive and subconcussive impacts (in terms of frequency and intensity). Therefore, those athletes most likely to get these brain diseases are those with 'bad' genes, either passed down by family members (called heredity) or due to chance (called genetic mutation), in combination with how much repetitive head trauma the athlete has had (again both in terms of amount over time and/or degree of injury). This means that some athletes are more at risk than others to suffer such consequences, for example, those having family histories of Alzheimer's, and those who have had exposure to severe (or multiple) concussions or flurries of A-SCBs injuries. This is one reason why this author is so passionate about spreading the world globally for youth to never to play head hurt, as it is the equivalent of throwing gas on a fire in terms of increasing a youth's degree of brain injury (brains already damaged AND more vulnerable because of not being fully mature).

Key Bottom Line(s): One of the bottom lines for the Big-3 is that many families don't know their medical histories back more than a generation or two, and there is always that wild card gene combination of genetic mutation. Another bottom line is that originally, this chapter reviewed no less than 10 major articles from peer reviewed journals on this subject, book content which was deferred because it was too technical and unnecessary overkill. Most of these articles suggested that the brain's hippocampus, specifically damaged by repetitive head injury, may be responsible for the symptoms of these chronic diseases and why they are disproportionately observed in athletes.

Conclusion: Now before anyone panics and pulls his or her child from a team or sport based on this black cloud of long-term consequences, it needs to be emphasized that we are only at the beginning of understanding the science around all of this. The silver lining is that BPE Youth gets young athletes started very early on the brain wellness best practices path. And readers may recall the brain's hippocampus and amygdala, both selectively damaged by repetitive head trauma, experience targeted functional improvement from specific BPE brain wellness best practices. The gold lining is that preventing or reducing concussion risk by avoiding concussions and A-SCBs in the first place is the absolute ideal scenario to prelude or eliminate long-term youth head injury consequences.

In closing, I would propose those brain health best practices that reduce chronic inflammation and oxidative stress, and which also increase the cell number/.volume and functioning of the hippocampus, are the best hedge solutions for helping prevent, ameliorate or delay the long-term brain damage consequences of repetitive head injury. And speaking of prevention, this next chapter describes two of the most innovative approaches for avoiding catastrophic head injuries and multiple concussions in ice-hockey, one old and one new. Their originators are collaborating to leverage the extreme value of their individual approaches to produce exponential head injury safety improvement outcomes.

Post Script August 26, 2014: As if by divine intervention, an hour before this book was final-approved for publication on August 26, 2014 several national media outlets reported Missouri State's Michael Keck, who died in 2013 at age 25 after playing only 2 years of college football, was found on brain autopsy to have the most severe case of CTE discovered thus far in a young athlete. Michael Keck's sports head injury story as reported by the Associated Press is another wake up call for us all – he is survived by his wife Cassandra and son Justin.

CHAPTER FOURTEEN

Heads Up, Don't Duck
& Look-Up Line
Preventing Paralysis, Second Impact Syndrome,
& Severe Concussions In Ice-Hockey

"You miss 100% of the shots you don't take." – Wayne Gretzky

Dr. Alan Ashare, this book's second author and Brain In Play's Chief Physician Concussion Adviser, first originated the *Heads Up, Don't Duck* program for USA Hockey back in the mid-1990s to prevent catastrophic head injuries (broken necks) and severe concussions as a result of hockey players crashing into the boards with their heads ducked down. A team physician and a student of advanced physics and biomechanics before and after medical school, Dr. Ashare knew that going head-first into the boards at no more than walking speed can produce a broken neck and paralysis—something he came face-to-face with in college hockey when his friend Boston University hockey player Travis Roy broke his neck during his first collegiate shift on the ice after being checked from behind. The previous summer Travis had lived at Dr. Ashare's home while skating for an elite team.

As USA Hockey's National Safety Committee Director and a tireless international sports safety advocate, Dr. Ashare foresaw with the Heads Up, Don't Duck program, the opportunity to prevent both mega-concussions and catastrophic paralyzing head/neck injuries by training youth hockey players from day one to lift their heads up when they recognized they were about to crash head-first into the boards that surround indoor ice rinks. While the program has had some success in hockey and has been adapted by other sports, Dr. Ashare spent years teaching that at least two improvement opportunities existed for his "heads-up" innovation. First and foremost, he was concerned that players could only be 100 percent successful at proactively lifting their heads if they recognized in time that they were about to hit the boards. This is not such an easy thing in hockey, when you are often looking down at a puck while traveling on skates at the highest speeds known to pedestrian sports. That both the ice and the boards are white makes heads-up recognition even more challenging. Second, with human nature being what it is, since one's natural reaction when bracing for a head-first crash while going fast is to duck down, players needed constant reminders for best heads-up success—what we call continuous cueing in behavioral health.

With regard to these core improvement opportunities, Dr. Ashare came across the solution in 2013 that, incredibly enough after almost twenty years of brainstorming, would seem to perfectly address both, big-time: The Look-Up Line™ (LUL). He quickly called a guy named Tom Smith.

Originated by former Massachusetts hockey star Thomas Smith who suffered two separate paralyzing accidents caused by crashing into the boards, the idea for a hockey rink-warning track first surfaced when Tom watched an MLB outfielder slow down and protect himself after reaching the field's warning track. The Look-Up Line™ is ice hockey's first warning track designed to reduce the risk of catastrophic and concussive head and neck injuries.

The Look-Up Line™ is a forty-inch wide track colored "safety orange" that extends around the entire circumference of a hockey rink. It serves to both remind and warn players to position their heads upward as they approach the boards. The line provides players enough visual reaction time to be aware that the boards are fast approaching so they can quickly begin to adjust their heads and bodies as they see orange coming into their peripheral vision. Further, everyone can see this orange line (see picture just below) as soon as they walk into any arena with a Look-Up Line™ rink—a consistent prompt to all stakeholders that it's about lifting your head when a crash into the boards is unavoidable. Another significant contribution of the LUL is to warn and remind players to be careful not to body check (contact) opposing players from behind when nearing the boards, especially when they are in vulnerable positions. Helping to take this form of checking off the table can only further reduce injury potential.

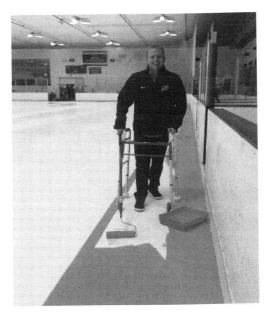

Tom Smith installs a <u>Look Up Line</u> at Phillips Academy Prep School in Andover, Massachusetts 2014

A quote from Tom Smith:

"The Look-Up Line is a thought provoking tool designed to de-crease the risk of catastrophic head and neck injuries in hockey. Right now hockey is in a state of crisis, as the retire-ment premise for players is all too often becoming catastrophic head, neck or severe concussive injuries. A big contributor to this problem is that players have outgrown the existing archi-tectural framework of hockey rinks. The Look-Up Line is a step in the right direction in modifying the playing surface to help keep up with the speed and growth of players. Put very simply, I do not want any player to have their career suddenly end and their life change like mine did. The Look-Up Line helps de-crease the risk of such a tragedy."

The good news for hockey purists is that the line does not affect the speed, intensity, or heritage of the game of hockey, nor does it re-quire any new playing rules directed at players. It makes the game of hockey safer for participants of all ages as a matter of course without affecting much else—including interfering with any of hockey's other ice markings, such as face-off dots, circles, or hash marks. And in terms of expense, adding this orange warning track can only be de-scribed as negligible—essentially what the paint costs.

As it turns out for hockey, Tom Smith's orange Look-Up Line™ is the quintessential or perfect add-on reminder to help the Heads-Up—Don't Duck program to be more consistently implemented, helping to prevent players from suffering catastrophic paralyzing spinal cord in-juries or major concussions. And Tom Smith is a big proponent of the necessity of continuous reminders, given his knowledge of hockey's intensity and his personal injury experience. This advocacy came through when he and I got into a discussion about something that be-came popular some years ago to address concerns about poor sportsmanship and overly aggressive play in high school sports. It had game officials bringing coaches and team captains together just before games started so that referees could remind team leadership that the biggest reason everyone was there was to compete in a spirit of fair play and good sportsmanship. We could add to this a brief tag-on about brain safety, such as:

"And remember, coaches and captains, the brain is the most important body part and is in play 24-7, so let's all do what we can as team leaders to avoid head injuries during our game to-day, on behalf of all players on the ice—and their parents and coaches as well."

This can make a huge difference, another healthy continuous reminder or cue to all that does not change games but sets the tone for avoiding dangerously aggressive play that could place youth players at undue risk for head or brain injuries. It also introduces some neutral pregame accountability to those who are closest to the action.

In closing, countless serious hockey injuries have been and will continue to be prevented by Heads Up, Don't Duck. There will just be even more avoided now because of the LUL. The marriage of the Heads Up, Don't Duck and Look-Up Line™ (LUL) initiatives is a classic example of out-of-the-box entrepreneurial thinking that spans across two generations, and integrates the key injury prevention ideas of a hockey safety physician advocate and a young thought-leading former star player (who was 5 years old when *'Head's Up'* was first originated). Without changing the game of hockey, these two individuals shared their core safety ideas in egoless fashion and joined forces to leverage their relationships of significance and influence change to improve hockey in general and youth hockey in particular.

This is exactly the kind of selfless collaboration that will be required to scientifically address and offset the worrisome new acute and longer term consequences of head injuries learned about in previous chapters, and why the Big-3 survival guides coming up next will be particularly helpful until then.

CHAPTER FIFTEEN

Survival Guides Introduction
Player Survival Guide

*"The question isn't who is going to let me;
it's who is going to stop me"~ Aya Rand*

General Introduction to Survival Guides

It should be clear to the reader by now that the Big-3, led by players, supported by parents and guided by coaches, comprise the key threesome who can turn around the sports head injury challenge most quickly and effectively with BPE-Youth and its Honor Code. Honoring the Code and pledging as many BPE best-brain wellness practices as possible is the most important thing any youth player can do to help win this war against youth sports head injuries **NOW** and going forward, regardless of what future neuroscience researchers discover.

To the often heard recent saying from some concussion experts: *"No evidence of brain damage that shows up on DTI scans can be good,"* let us add, *"Nothing all-natural that improves the functioning, preservation, and growth of healthy brain cells can be bad, especially if combined with a player-led Code of Honor that helps protect youth brains and hardwires integrity around never playing head-hurt."*

The extent to which players, parents, and coaches can work together in support of BPE-Youth and its Honor Code will in large part determine the success of ASAP youth sports head injury risk reduction, healing, and consequence avoidance. This is whether talking about individual cases with single youth/parent/coach triads, individual team situations, school or league-wide opportunities, or even larger organizational or community efforts.

It is also likely that to the extent expert concussion care providers can be involved to provide guidance and/or consultation to these change-management improvement process scenarios, community and organizational successes will be greatly enhanced. In addition, there will be heightened potential for year-to-year continuity and expansion of BPE-Youth initiatives to even more players, parents, and coaches— key seedlings for growth. This will be especially so if these expert providers connect strongly with senior star athletes to improve the chances these *youth athlete icons* can be retained to carry the message along to other youth following in their footsteps in the year(s) to come—in person.

While the term "survival guide" does imply an ultimate challenge scenario, which some may say is inflammatory, let's be reminded of two recent events previously mentioned in this book, one involving 200 USA-Hockey coaches and one involving a player and his parents. Before presenting BPE Youth to USA Hockey's top Level 4 coaches we confidentially surveyed them and 95% indicated needing to learn more about concussions, with 90% also confirming they were very worried about sports head injuries. Considering the amount of high quality training these Level-4 coaches have had, this was telling.

The other event involved our teenage sophomore rising star football player Joe from Chapter eight, with severe post-concussion syndrome and highly educated parents who found us totally by accident. They had just been to a top provider that had prescribed total cognitive rest, and not much else from parental report. The youth's school was a top private high school whose football teacher-coach wasn't happy a star player was missing most of the season and began avoiding him. By the time Joe got to us, he was so depressed he nearly required hospitalization, and his mother, a top executive leader, was so angry she talked of quitting her job to become a youth concussion advocate. Joe's depression had been playing out for weeks and two of his teachers (one in particular) seemed to think he was embellishing his cognitive symptoms, making his depression worse.

It took a few sessions, but with a combination of BPE and some aggressive cognitive therapy, Joe's depression lifted and his other symptoms began improving significantly. What this young man needed most was a solid therapeutic relationship, and his parents just needed to adjust a few things on their end, that the previous provider's fifteen-minute or less check-ins weren't uncovering. Brief check-ins (which included having the parent and player fill out a concussion symptom check-list prior to being seen) may work for diabetes or other disease management checks, and might be alright for adults post-concussion, but are not clinically sufficient for teens. Building relationships that uncover symptoms like lethal suicide, or that drive high levels of sustained motivation require more in depth contact.

In our experience, these two types of scenarios just described involving youth players, parents and coaches are not unusual (recall national sports figure Briana Scurry's earlier quote regarding her four year challenge to get the right concussion help). Concussion survival mode is not unusual particularly for teens and their families; in fact we hear about them almost every day. In combination with sophisticated coaches who have had basic concussion training but are telling the world it isn't enough, there can be no question we must do more. And given that, to be more successful, changes are in the wind that require new ways of behaving and taking on some strong and longstanding cultural forces in sports, I think the term "survival guides" is fitting.

Player Survival guide

1. **BPE-Youth Honor Code First Up**: Most player survival guide recommendations center on changing *how* a youth athlete does what she/he does. Not surprisingly, the top survival priority 'how' is never playing head hurt. Ignoring this priority is the quickest and most reliable way to get a more serious injury, which in the least means more lost playing time from a more lengthy recovery. In worst cases, this could lead to a treatment-resistant post-concussive syndrome lasting years or to a second impact syndrome. If you are head-hurt you are not at your athletic best, for yourself, your team or your coach. The Code of Honor and Behavior is the only answer here – remembering that it's a lot harder and takes a lot more guts and courage to be strong enough to sit out than it does to be tough enough to play when hurt.

2. **BPE Brain Wellness Best Practices is Next Up**: How players manage their lives so brain inflammation and toxic oxidants are minimized, while immunity, healing reserves and other forms of bran cell resilience are maximized, is the next priority "how" of player survival. The BE-CHAMPS 24/7 acronym's most telling message is about the brain being in play at all hours of the day/night seven days a week, with athletic performance excellence and injury-avoidance being about more than pregame meals and great practice weeks. A reminder: The BE CHAMPS 24/7 six best practice categories consistently integrates all your brain power to work at top levels, keeping you hyper-alert to better recognize when those big hits are coming and positioning your head and body to 'automatically' respond in ways that help minimize your chances of a head injury outcome. Now that we know we have much more control over quickly changing our brain structure and function (by combining those two new sciences of epigenetics and neuroplasticity) it is a matter of committing to as many of these routines as possible that improve the functioning, preservation and growth of brain cells.

3. **Perfection is Not the Goal with BPE Best Practices**: Athletes don't have to be perfect at doing all BE-CHAMPS brain wellness practices consistently 100% (although for world class athletes who are serious about getting to the next level of their sport, this is definitely worth striving for). The best approach is to do as many as possible, starting with the easiest ones to work into your lifestyle, taking notice about how much better and more focused you are and

how your athletic and academic performance improves. If you have a concussion history or play a high risk sport like football, hockey, soccer or lacrosse, regarding BE-CHAMPS – 24/7: "Just Do It!"

4. **Playing Smart**: Most concussions and more intense A-SCBs take place during games, with big game situations being particularly high-risk. It therefore makes sense for youth players to take a step back and plan for how to limit the potential for concussions and flurries of A-SCBs from happening. The chapter featuring "Heads Up, Don't Duck and the Look Up Line" was in part included to help drive this point home. Visualizing those high-risk head injury game situations before playing gives you a chance to rehearse and think through how to best keep your head up should those scenarios occur. Practicing these types of defensive maneuvers on one's own in live situations is another common sense way to prep for avoiding head injuries. And while primarily a coaching responsibility, players thinking through how concussions and intense A-SCBs can be limited in practices is yet another way smart play can reduce sports head injuries. These types of injuries have much to do with head hit counts, as we now know that the more often, and the more intense A-SCBs are for high school and college contact sports players, the more damaged their brains look on DTI scans.

5. **After A Concussion**: If you are early in a recovery from a concussion, access a knowledgeable expert concussion provider; one that plans to spend at least 30 minutes with you. The provider should convey to you and your parent a sincere sense of trust and interest in your specific case, ask lots of questions, and really listen to your concerns, at least 50% of the time. A check in with your parent while you are there is a must (the reality is you have been brain injured and providers should always confirm your report of symptoms with a family member). This is recommended whether you are having active symptoms or not, as there is evidence now that at least 4 months after a concussion white matter damage persists whether you have symptoms or not, and <u>absolutely necessary if you have a history of previous concussion</u>(s). When your parent calls the specialist's office in advance and the response is not consistent with either an MD, or licensed independent Psychologist or Nursing Clinical Specialist trained in concussion/brain injury care spending at least 30 minutes with you, than find someone else in your area. This minimum length of time is necessary to confirm clinical assessment and to form a trusting therapeutic relationship. This is essential given

new research evidence-basis for cognitive restructuring improving hippocampal growth, as well to have the opportunity to share the details of your specific case without being rushed (remembering that every concussion is different than the next).

6. **Return to School and Play**: Plan to take more time off from sports than you ordinarily would and don't return to full time traditional classroom activities or sports until symptoms have completely resolved and you have been cleared by a qualified specialist. As you return to sports, do so in a graded and gradual way. Recall that the issue of accumulated sub-concussive blows is more dangerous than previously thought. Having talked with the parents of high profile second impact syndrome cases, I am becoming convinced that while a second concussion is clearly a precipitant or final event that may lead to this fatal brain swelling, a flurry of A-SCBs can cause this also. Regarding school, with severe post-concussion syndrome you will need accommodations or special help. If you aren't usually assertive asking for help, *become your own advocate*, as this is your brain, and getting a concussion wasn't your fault. Help is truly necessary when returning to academics. Being able to handle school and sports transitions gradually is a sign of maturity and will help you actually get back to a normal brain/life sooner without the risk of undeservedly lower grades and chancing catastrophic brain damage. This is even more important for those with a past history of multiple concussions or recovering from a severe concussion.

7. **More Emotional Than Usual or Feeling Down or Depressed**: A high percentage of post-concussed HS/College athletes suffer depression or experience more extreme emotions. This is a normal biological result of concussion, from those selectively damaged regions of the brain's gray matter that process emotions. If you begin to feel increasingly depressed or sad, share this immediately with an adult you trust (preferably a parent) who can get you to professional help. The best news about depression is that it is a highly treatable concussion complication. Four of BPE-Youth's best practices markedly improve most depressions, including breathing to focus, endurance exercise, cortisol reduction and sleep hygiene. Abstaining from alcohol and marijuana also helps, given drugs that are psychoactive, depress the brain or kills its cells worsens this condition. Cognitive behavioral restructuring will likely be the prescribed therapy, which beyond fostering hippocampal brain cell growth, improves depression's core symptoms as well.

8. **BPE Youth Improves Coach Communication**: While not necessarily in the category of survival mode, letting your coach know of your BPE Youth Fast-Track involvement will help improve your mutual connectedness. In the least it is a conversation starter that lets him/her know you are serious about injury avoidance and sports/academic performance enhancement. BPE-Youth can also be used as a way to let coaches know how you are managing your concussion recovery, or what you are doing regarding prevention maintenance, should you be a returning high school or college junior/senior with a history of multiple concussions. This may help improve a coach's comfort level with relating to you around this issue, and with assigning you more playing time when appropriate.

9. **BPE Youth and Getting to the Next Level**: In terms of doing everything possible to get to the next level, there is no question that leveraging BPE Youth to avoid head injuries and to enhance athletic and academic performance will help. Whether your intention is to transition from being a part time to a full time player or from high school to college athletics, getting a coach's attention with a self-management improvement program and then delivering better athletic performance works. And using BPE Youth's Honor Code to show that you have integrity and team leadership qualities are yet another opportunity that BPE-Youth presents to athletes working to differentiate themselves from others.

In closing this survival guide, the bottom line for youth athletes involves realizing that while sports head injuries are becoming higher profile in most middle/high school and college sports venues, it is only going to become an even hotter issue going forward. This is not something to shy away from, as it is here to stay. A great win-win strategy is to take a leadership role on this issue at your school or on your team. Your brain is your most precious body part, whether talking sports, academics, relationships, your future or life in general.

CHAPTER SIXTEEN

A Survival-Enhancement Guide for Parents

"Life is not measured by the number of breaths we take, but by the moments that take our breath away." ~ *Maya Angelou*

Introduction: For parents and youth sports head injuries, failing to plan is planning to fail. If your child is playing a contact sport, it is prudent to have a clear plan for how you will manage the potential for head injury. It is especially important if your child has a history of previous concussion or if the child or coaching situation suggests a need to be more vigilant than usual (a sports-aggressive child playing a high-risk sport or that rare concussion-unaware/dismissive coach).

Intelligent advance planning is a parent's strong suit as a member of the Big-3 for two reasons. First, there will never be a stronger advocate for a youth athlete than a parent. Best advocacy is about being proactive and making sure nothing is overlooked, underestimated, or missed—almost always the root cause of why bad things happen regarding sports head injuries. Second, and just as critical, no one knows a child better than a parent, and head injuries can be incredibly subtle—meaning that in some cases a parent is the best judge of whether a head or body impact has had a concussive effect on a player. Taking this one step further, a highly tuned-in parent may notice a change related to brain trauma that the affected child doesn't even perceive. I have observed this in my clinical work and as a coach.

Once while managing a college freshman all-star baseball team, I had a parent approach me at the end of an inning to say her son, my all-star catcher, didn't seem quite right. His mom relayed to the dugout that he wasn't walking around the way he usually does after strikeout outs were recorded during the inning before. There had been a moderate collision some innings earlier at home plate, and both managers went on the field to confirm all parties were okay, which they were at the time. As it turned out, a major headache was beginning (3 innings later) that, until I pulled him aside, the player didn't even notice! We learned he had suffered his third concussion and ended up missing most of the season—diagnosed from the stands by his mother two hundred feet away.

[1] Once thought to be brain-safe, soccer causes white and gray matter brain damage and ranks among the highest risk concussion/A-SCBs sports

Parent Survival Guide

1. **The Honor Code**: If there is interest, encourage your child to consider leading the way with the youth sports head injury Code of Honor and Behavior, but don't force him or her—just don't seem disinterested when it might come up. This is the primary way head injuries can be avoided, or should they happen, be managed as well as possible. Playing head-hurt is by far the biggest risk all kids face. Plan for how you will respond ahead of time, so when this issue comes up, you are not taken off guard. See later for how to engage with coaches around this issue.

2. **Have A Parent Plan**: Parents of contact sports athletes need to have a comprehensive plan with contingencies to observe their kids. At a bare minimum, this should include making sure someone is always watching your child, especially during games—as this is when most concussions happen. Recall the previous mantra: watch your child like a hawk. If it can't always be a parent, a relative or best friend substitute should be asked. It bears repeating that coaches, no matter how good can't and don't see everything. Even if they could, concussive symptoms are sometimes so subtle and variable from player to player that only someone who knows the child can tell by observing from afar. The degree to which heroic efforts are considered, such as taking time out of work to attend games, should relate to the degree of risk posed by a given child's situation (e.g., has the child suffered a previous concussion during the past year? Is this a multiply concussed high school quarterback? Is this a forward on a premier girls soccer team who will be marked by the opposing team's best defensive player with a history of yellow/red cards?).

3. **School/League Parent Nights**: Many schools and leagues now have parent nights at the beginning of seasons. Attend them and expect to hear about and see in writing a comprehensive sports head injury management plan with specifics regarding how a coaching staff will handle suspected concussions. This plan should minimally include notification of parent, sideline assessment by a healthcare practitioner, emergency transport to nearest ER, and clearance from a concussion-knowledgeable LIP before return to play (and never on same day). If you don't see or hear this, be forceful and ask about what the school or league's sports head injury policy is, and request a copy. Thanks to cell phones, you can always take a picture of what policy you are shown. If you have any concerns, you can compare it to those American Academy of Neurology primers previously men-

tioned and print them down from the www.AAN.com website to share with school or coaching personnel.

4. **Inquire About School/League Head Injury Reduction Plan:** Now that school officials are wondering who you are, inquire about the school or league policy/plan regarding risk reduction for both concussions and A-SCBs. The response should be one of acknowledgment, and in the least, show practice accommodations are being made that significantly reduces the frequency of unnecessary contact. The reason we focused on soccer in Chapter six is that for many basketball, hockey, and baseball/softball playing youth, it is now the fall cross training sport of choice (previously thought to be benign and now known to be high risk for head injuries)—and heading soccer balls in practice should not be allowed. Recall that even moderate impacts can cause A-SCBs or concussions if they involve quick acceleration/decelerations of the head and/or rotations of the skull, both of which cause axons to stretch beyond their capacity and break. Needless to say, players having had a concussion in the past year are at greatest risk.

5. **Know The 'Go To' Reference Guides**: Select and consult quick reference guides often. Take time to review the www.CDC.gov. "Heads Up Concussion" website, usually required by most schools and leagues. Also freely use the www.BrainInPlay.com youth sports website as a tool that has hot links to excellent other references. Also our website offers many of the latest youth sports head injury research updates.

6. **Use BPE Fast-Track to Improve Communication at Home**: Become a collaborative BPE partner with your student athlete. This means walking that fine line between being involved enough as a parent and not getting overinvolved in your child's sports life. This is best managed by keeping the lines of communication open and clarifying as much as possible your Big-3 parental role up front and at regular intervals with your child (something the Code of Honor can be leveraged for). Proactively discuss what your child thinks the correct parental response should be if you suspect a concussive injury. Approaching things this way more often than not opens more doors to communication with your student athlete and ensures that nothing important is left unsaid. And be as BPE Youth Fast-Track supportive as your children allow and you are comfortable with. Look over the BPE Youth best practices, and evaluate if you might be a poor example for any of these Fast-Track six. They apply to

individuals of any age; the top brain wellness best practices that, when aggregated, will improve the functioning, preservation, and growth of brain cells (and body cells too). Consider being a model for your youth athlete on these best brain wellness practices.

7. **Use BPE Youth to Improve Communication with Coaches**: If possible, become a collaborative concussion reduction partner with your child's coaching staff. There needs to be clear understanding around boundaries (you just report what you see/know, and the coaching staff investigates). Many coaches in this day and age welcome parental support and proactive communication. Most are smart enough to understand when they are being approached by a parent that can help. Just passing along the AAN one-page primers/apps would be a big advantage if they are unfamiliar with them. By now, most parents have figured out that the Code of Honor and Behavior is as helpful to parents and coaches as it is for youth. While the ultimate Code outcome specifically benefits youth athletes by preventing or minimizing the severity of head injuries, it also acts to create a cultural bond between parents and coaches (and kids) who are now expected to be collaborators rather than parties to be avoided. It's all about the kids—period. Learning how to best leverage this newfound parent/coach/athlete tool is a priority.

8. **When Concussions Happen:** In the event of concussion, have your child evaluated by an emergency medical team as soon as possible. While unlikely that a life threatening consequence is pending, with head impacts this is always possible (brain bleeding, brain swelling, or skull fracture) so take no chances. Hospital emergency rooms are preferable (open 24/7 with top imaging equipment). Once medically cleared engage a qualified concussion specialist for a comprehensive assessment. Locate specialists nearby who will spend time with your child (at least thirty minutes) and involve you in the process. This is the best way that three 'must-have' things can happen:

➤ Subtleties with your child's head injury can be uncovered;

➤ Depression can be evaluated (kids won't reveal unless they trust);

➤ A therapeutic relationship develops that leverages brain cell growth.

9. **Return to academics and play is always a parental challenge**. The highest risk situation for post-concussed players is to return to the classroom or sports too soon. And we have new information about this courtesy of those DTI scans mentioned in Chapter six –

'just because a youth athlete doesn't have symptoms doesn't mean there isn't brain damage'. And while we don't yet fully understand the clinical implications of this research, *the obvious take-away is to be more conservative about return to school/play until we do*. In the case of academics, a premature return to class can be taxing and delays healing, or even worsen brain dysfunction or damage (recall that too much cortisol from stress further impairs brain cell functioning and prevents new growth). Regarding premature return to sports, that's why we designed BPE's Honor Code, as to risk playing head hurt invites the possibility of worst-case scenarios and there is but only one hyphenated phrase for that: **zero-tolerance**. Finally on return to academics/play, we remind you check out Dr. Ashare's colleague Dr. Gerry Gioia's work[17] in this area, for which he received a lifetime achievement award by the Sports Legacy Institute in April of 2014. An associated tangible resource for a five-phase return to school can be found on the Nationwide Children's Hospital site under concussion clinic resources at:

www.nationwidechildrens.org.

More return to school and play information is also readily available at:http://www.cdc.gov/concussion/headsup/pdf/ACE_care_plan_sch ool_version_a.pdf

Depression and Behavioral Health: *The need for parents to be vigilant regarding post-concussive depression and suicidal thinking can't be emphasized enough.* The rate of suicides in post-concussed teens and young adults is shocking and stems from the previously mentioned selective damage to mood stabilization and emotional control centers in the brain, on top of post-traumatic stresses and losses that come with being a head injured athlete. If you suspect depression is happening with your child get them to a qualified (concussion) provider trained in both behavioral and brain health and who routinely treats adolescents and college students. Since this is such a significant and scientifically proven consequence, Brain In Play is adding "post sports head injury depression/suicidal behavior[11] to the list of catastrophic outcomes involved with concussions and A-SCBs.

CHAPTER SEVENTEEN

Coaches Survival Guide

"Few things can help an individual more than to place responsibility on him, and to let him know that you trust him"

~ Booker T. Washington

Coaches of middle/high school and college youth sports teams have a major responsibility to act on the knowledge they have learned or had confirmed in this book. But first, let's not forget to applaud youth coaches for reading this book and all that they do to make youth sports happen oftentimes on a volunteer basis. Toward the end of my coaching career, I can remember racing from hospitals driving in traffic and changing in stadium parking lots, thinking at many points I should "throw in the towel", but was begged by one group of young men I had been coaching for 10 years, to stay on. From one coach to another, I understand the sacrifices coaches make and fully appreciate your attention on this matter. I also understand the enormous power and influence that many coaches have with student athletes. It is probably safe to say that most youth form their final opinions about sports head injuries from their coaches. In this regard by extension, it is also academic to say coaches will have much to say about the success of BPE-Youth's Honor Code and best-practices.

The ultimate sports head injury takeaway for coaches is to more fully understand, embrace and then walk the talk about one basic foundational principle that has eluded most of us day to day through our years of coaching: the brain is the most important body part determining the success and athletic performance of any player, across all sports. When we say players have heart, it is a misnomer. What they really have is an unwavering belief in self and loyalty to the team to always compete full speed (courtesy of the brain). When we marvel at how a player seems to have a nose for the ball/puck or an uncanny sense for the fundamentals, it's really that the player's brain has set this up to happen. When that one-handed catch is made while falling down, it's not soft hands or strong arms really, but what's called proprioception, a brain function that probably ties into thousands of brain cell regions and networks for this to happen perfectly in a game.

Why is it more necessary now for youth coaches to more fully understand the brain? We have learned more about brain functioning and development in relation to key biosciences that influence the brain (and athletic/academic performance) in the last two years than the previous century. Just as the passing game has become essential to football, the jump shot critical to scoring the basketball, and defensive infield shifts part of baseball, so are we learning top brain functioning is mission critical to all sports, especially when it comes to avoiding head injuries and getting top individual and team performances. A bottom line: we have used the cliché that knowledge is power, and to that we must add, taking responsibility and accountability is power.

Because players most often get what information they trust about head injuries from coaches, it is a coach's job to **protect, educate and serve** players around this issue. This is a daunting task considering much of the new DTI research flooding the sports world. That is why much of this coach's survival guide is a drill down on how to just do these 3 italicized things well, armed with BPE's Code of Honor and Behavior. Due to the latest DTI research, youth sports is becoming a whole new game coaches must deal with across all sports, and coaches had better get comfortable with changing their ways a bit. This includes being more open to changing up practice regimens and involving others who can help keep the players we coach as brain healthy as possible (i.e., players and parents). So let's begin the process by considering the following suggestions.

1. **Implement BPE's Honor Code**: The best thing for coaches about BIP International's sports head injury Honor Code is that it shares the responsibility for zero tolerance playing head-hurt between coaches and players. *It reframes the culture of sports from one of "gutting things out" to: Are you strong enough to sit it out when head hurt due to loyalty to the team and teammates, and out of honor to the brain and youth sports?* Getting parents involved in the process upfront is also a good idea, making the expectation clear that parents need to report any player symptoms to coaches right away. President Obama at his recent White House Summit stated it is a strong player who admits having a head injury. That may be, but absent a written coach supported values-driven Code of Honor and Behavior that players and parents sign, it is unlikely that high school or college players will buck the powerful unspoken and unwritten youth sports culture status quo, complicated more often than not by their own personal agendas (playing time, scholarships etc.). And while it hasn't happened yet large scale, it soon will – some parent or graduated student with a significant interest, right or wrong, will use litigation to hold a coach accountable for allegedly not protecting a brain injured player enough. *If I was coaching today how soon would I implement BPE's Honor Code? Yesterday!*

2. **Develop Your Captains**: Coaches must take more responsibility for player and coaching staff leadership development. Most youth players take their lead from coaches and upper classmen regarding what the *real* team values and honor/behavior code is. Many college and high-school coaches have long tenures, supporting this development process to have continuity. The key issue for coaches is consistency and alignment within your coaching staff and with team captains for how to respond to head injuries. Have a written policy and Code of Honor, keep them posted, remind constantly and never deviate.

3. **Improve Relationships and Communication with Parents**: What will become most essential for coach survival going forward (being successful and at peace) is having good relationships with parents.

Once thought to be unwise, "They are your kids before and after games/practices but my kids otherwise," sharing kids is no longer considered taboo by many coaches, particularly at the high school level. This doesn't mean there aren't boundaries, but it does mean with head injuries, or histories thereof, there is proactive communication between coaches and parents versus passivity or relying on notes from student athlete providers/parents. An easy way to hardwire good basic communication around sports head injuries is having parents sign on to BPE's Honor Code upfront.

4. **Hold Providers Accountable**: Coaches need to make sure they know who is medically signing off on players returning from a concussion. I was recently connected with one of the more esteemed hospitals in the region where a sports medicine physician was letting an experienced sports healthcare nonphysician/LIP 'type' make the decisions on safe return to play and then the MD would just sign off without ever seeing the player. This individual was fairly experienced but in the case of one player, my clinical team became aware of a missed critical medical nuance that most concussion experienced physicians or independent medical practitioners would have picked up in a heart-beat that placed the player, coach and team at risk (and needless to say the hospital). For the most part we are not talking about athletes of adult age here – these are youth brains that are more developmentally complicated and vulnerable out of the gate, even before a head injury happens. A coach should advocate for their head injured athletes to be clinically assessed by an MD or a credentialed licensed independent medical practitioner before returning to play. Have parents insist on it and not take no for an answer. This is the best way for coaches to serve and protect injured players.

5. **Integrate BPE Youth Into Practices**: Starting in middle school sports practices are usually for long periods of time after school every day during the week, extended to weekends in most high-schools and college. There is ample time to work in some BPE Youth Fast-Track practice priorities. Why should a coach consider this? For at least three good reasons:

• It's the right thing to do for best-practice head injury prevention, to help off-set A-SCBs and reduce concussion risk;

• It's a smart proactive thing to do from a liability perspective;

- It's the right and smart proactive thing to do to enhance player game performance and improve team play, and to improve academic eligibility.

What should be emphasized and possibly worked into practices?

1) Five minutes of controlled breathing and positive imagery at beginning or end of practices on M/W/Fri, with athletes envisioning individual and team success;
2) Reminders about smart meals and foods to avoid, especially pregame;
3) Continuous education re: value of sleep and dangers of alcohol and stress;
4) Focus on Code of Honor and Behavior: Student athletes need reminders and deserve a coach's best leadership;
5) Preach hydration and safety – specifically mentioning high-risk situations.
6) Work in these neck strengthening exercise regimens

All of these seemingly basic and simple things are hugely important when it comes to improving the functioning, preservation and growth of brain cells. Not a coach's job? In this day and age of coaching sports it most certainly is, core to the job in fact. A major upside of doing these things together as a team in practice is that it helps with team building and reinforces the Honor Code. Has a coaching version of this been done before successfully, and then replicated? We might want to ask former Bulls and Lakers Coach Phil Jackson about that— and how many championships did he win? And Jackson did it not once, but replicated it a second time for 2 sets of 3 championships!

Modify Practices and Practice Games to Limit A-SBCs/Concussions: There can be no question that with the new DTI research on A-SCBs that has been sufficiently replicated (which means the findings are new but have been confirmed by multiple rsearchers), that Athletic Directors and Head Coaches need to limit unnecessary jarring physical contact in practices that could be of sub-concussive quality. This of course also goes for 'pre and during season' practice games and scrimmages. When reloading on contact in practices and scrimmages err on the side of caution and consider reviewing your adjusted regimens with an objective concussion expert for feedback. Formally document that in consideration of the new head injury research on A-SCBs that you have modified your practices to reduce risk for both concussions and A-SCBs, and keep these records on file. Other suggestions include having sports head injury coaching retreats focused on improvement opportunities and inviting a concussion expert with coaching experience to facilitate, and consider attending regional/national conferences on this topic.

To conclude this survival primer for coaches we must reiterate the quintessential value coaches bring to the mission of reducing youth head injuries and best healing those that do happen. The Institute of Medicine Report was clear in its message that today's culture of youth sports often prevents head hurt players from accessing and finishing needed treatment. Worse still is the reality that despite awareness and education programs, the majority of head hurt athletes continue to play and hide symptoms from coaches and parents. Thus, coaching leadership is sorely needed and is perhaps the lynchpin game-changer in turning this emerging public health crisis around. We desperately need head coaches in all sports to step up, get totally educated, develop their coaching staffs and captains, and implement the Honor Code.

In closing BPE Youth Fast-Track is pleased to provide the coaching universe key best practices and culture change-management tools to help win the war against youth sports head injury as quickly as possible. Together, let's work to prevent, heal and avoid the consequences of these head injuries, while enhancing the athletic, academic and life performance of our student athletes.

CHAPTER EIGHTEEN

Going Viral: A Challenge to Dance for Players & Those Who Love Them

"How wonderful is it that nobody need wait a single moment before starting to improve the world" ~ *Anne Frank*

I have been told that it can't be done, that this generation of youth is more interested in their smart phones and acquiring things than helping people. I disagree totally. I believe that this decade of youth (12-22) is more genuinely interested in their friends and the worthwhile causes of others than the other 3 or 4 that I have experienced in my lifetime. I have observed this increased *caring about other people* and *willingness to take action* in my roles as a clinician-scientist, sports coach, and behavioral/brain health provider and parent. Many of my academic/professional peers chuckle and say what I am applauding about this group is intangible. In response, I ask them to use their eyes and ears to do more than look and hear, but to observe and listen to what is happening around us. Most middle/high-school and college age youth use smart phones to text, tweet, call and more, in order to stay connected with friends and others they genuinely care about. The integration of the internet with social media has provided more awareness about various causes that would have previously gone unnoticed by 'youth', most of whom don't watch TV news or read newspapers/RSS feeds.

What am I ranting about? I'm talking about the real possibility of quickly changing the culture of youth sports regarding head injuries, with the help of youth athletes and those who care about them. This starts with athletes pledging to follow as many of BPE Youth's brain wellness best-practices as possible and committing to BPE's Honor Code. We are then asking youth/supporters to text, tweet, make You-Tubes, log onto Facebook, call up friends, upload Instagram photos/vidoes (this book cover etc.), and/or email everyone you are connected with about this book and that it offers brain/life-saving brain wellness best practices and an Honor Code. *"Take the Brain In Play Pledge and Honor the Code."* Let players, parents and coaches in your world and around the globe know they can immediately download this as an E-Book with a Kindle App for under $10 or purchase the hard copy from Amazon Books for under $15...less than the cost of a couple of sandwiches, or 3-4 large beverages 'to go' in the U.S.!

Doing this is called *disruptive innovation* by Clayton Christensen, the world's top thought leader regarding radical systems change that happens when committed individuals *'find out about a new and better way'*, and the buzz spreads to huge numbers of others who also benefit. Ultimately, you will be sharing how to best prevent sports head injuries and enhance athletic, academic and life performance with best practices quickly helping athletes to be more brain-sharp. The greatest reward is that beyond improving the brains and lives of youth athletes some will be saved, and large numbers of post-concussive brain disabilities will be prevented or minimized.

The priceless BPE Youth Honor Code outcome is that no head hurt player will ever be left in danger, behind or forgotten; a rather honorable cause to support, and one that when it spreads large-scale, the sports world will stand up and take notice. Together we will have made a big difference in reducing youth sports head injuries by changing the culture of sports and brain health, and adding an evidence-based brain wellness premise to the care mix. As success happens, a portion of this book's proceeds will be donated to the foundations of those players' who families have generously chosen to honor the lives of their catastrophically injured beloved athletes by helping raise awareness so that other youth players may avoid a similar experience.

So enough writing, discussion, and calls for action about the youth sports head injury issue. We now have a dual way to make sports safer and to save the sports that most middle/high school and college athletes love to play, AND that helps prevent and heal head injuries.

We reduce the risk of sports head injuries and restore brain health after concussion and A-SCBs with BPE Youth Fast-Track, and we use BPE Youth's Honor Code to prevent youth from playing head hurt and support needed treatment access if injured. Both BPE Youth innovations work best in tandem with one other. This being said we need to blueprint two things for this to happen most quickly.

#1. Systematically spread the word about the BPE Youth movement with a dance challenge led by players and supporters.

This is the first time in history that youth athletes (and those who love them) have been in a position to change something so big and so important about sports. Never before have so many youth 21ish and under had the committed spirit and know-how to make a national and global change initiative happen, armed with the communication tools and technological abilities to do it, *right in the palms of their hands.*

We are talking of course about the smart phone, internet and social media networks. After reading this book one has the necessary BPE Youth knowledge to make a brain saving difference just by communicating to others what the key youth sports head injury priorities are:

A. **Don't play head hurt** – *Do Brain In Play's Honor Code*

B. **Be a head-strong player** – *Do Brain In Play's Best Practices*

The "Going Viral" chapter title believes youth can achieve everything from team, school or city-wide communication, to state, national and global messaging by combining music, dance and social media talents. Our youth 'blueprinting' student athlete consultants advise spreading Brain In Play's mantras **A & B** highlighted in gray above in **Dance-Challenge You Tubes**. Just as the ALS Ice Bucket Challenge was spread virally by adults in the summer of 2014, youth athletes and loving supporters can improve the brains/lives of multiple millions by posting dances and inviting others to take the ***Brain In Play Concussion Dance Challenge*** – keeping it respectful and fun of course! Who will have the top '***Honor Code or Head Strong Brain In Play***' dance video: guys versus young ladies, middle or high-school versus college teams, a middle-school Phenom, perhaps even a celebrity or two might join in. And it will be hard to keep talented parents, coaches and others from dancing for this great ***brain and life-saving cause***. As most of this book's quotes suggest, it's time to stop being silent!

For those not so inclined to dance, some more traditional ways to spread the word, depending on preference, time and resources:

- Become an ambassador and create a YouTube Video explaining to other youth athletes about the dangers of playing brain hurt and the useful information that this book has helped you with. You can become an important relay and role model that helps save lives! Send along any testimonials to Brain In Play's Facebook page.
- Tweet or text and remind players and friends before 'Game Day' to pass the word by tweeting/texting about BPE's Honor Code of not playing when head-hurt, and practicing some of BPE Youth's best practices as a preseason or pregame routine.
- Join our Call to Action page on Facebook, invite others to join our Facebook page and start engaging in weekly topics of conversation and important updates on sports head injury and brain wellness. Feel free to post thoughts, ask questions or start a discussion.

- We will re-tweet your tweets, share classic videos and respond on Facebook. If we all put our hands and heads into this cause like a team does on a field, rink, pitch, track, court etcetera, we can create real culture change almost overnight together!
- So knowing all it takes today for earth-shaking global change is to ask the right individuals who care to stand up and help spread the message, and provide those people basic ways about what and how to communicate, here are some possible twitter messaging scripts:

  ➢ #1Seller: New sports concussion book 4all2 change R life + get U bigger/better brain @ www.BrainInPlay.com
  ➢ #1Seller: War on youth concussions book has honor-code: no head hurt player left in danger, behind/forgotten @ www.BrainInPlay.com
  ➢ #1 book helps prevent/heal concussions 4 middle/high-school/college players + enhances athletics @ www.BrainInPlay.com
  ➢ Takes way more strength+guts 2 sit if head-hurt than it does 2 B tough enough 2 play injured. B ice-cool@ www.BrainInPlay.com

#2. A Big-3 crowd-sourcing feedback loop

We have created a crowd-sourcing feedback loop for the Big-3 to provide input on how this book and BPE Youth Fast-Track can be improved. Provide ideas on how we can better get the message out about the BPE Youth movement, so more youth athletes can avoid sports brain damage; and even fewer will play head-hurt, so as many catastrophic injuries as possible can be prevented and no head-injured youth athlete will ever be left in danger, behind or forgotten. **We suggest Brain In Play's Facebook page and welcome all of your input with sincerest appreciation.**

Conclusion

"Great moments are born from great opportunity. And that's
what you have here tonight...if we played 'em 10 times they
might beat us 9...but not tonight, not tonight!
You were born [for this moment]...Now go out and take it!"

~ Herb Brooks, Coach 1980 Olympic Men's Hockey Team
Pre-Game Speech, USA versus Russia 'Miracle on Ice Game'

It is difficult to conclude this book about **Youth Sports Head Injuries**, a red-hot issue representing the most serious public health crisis facing U.S. youth today, soon to emerge globally as an alarming cause of brain damage given DTI research in process on youth soccer (world's most popular sport played by almost 300 million). But conclude we must, laser-focused on co-prioritizing the two critical follow-ups the Big-3 and all others who care about youth athletes should leave this book thinking hard about and taking action on:

♦ **preventing any middle/high-school and college athlete from ever participating in practices or games while head hurt;**
♦ **sharing whatever news we can today in support of players and their brains being safer for the sports they play.**

BPE Youth's Code of Honor/Behavior and Best Practices together comprise a quick-win comprehensive strategy, which gives the Big-3 the necessary tools to *immediately* address both follow-ups, and begin winning the war against youth sports head injuries. These dual innovations ultimately fine-tune the culture of youth sports zeroed in on *sports head injury prevention, healing and consequence avoidance.*

What is necessary to achieve and sustain this youth sports culture improvement involves recognizing and incentivizing four core beliefs:

> ➢ **When head hurt, it takes a lot more courage to be strong enough to sit out, than it does to be tough enough to play.**
> ➢ **To be the best performing athlete one can be the most important body part to get and keep in shape is The Brain.**
> ➢ **24/7 brain wellness is the best hedge to prevent and heal head injuries, and improve athletic and school performance.**
> ➢ **No Big-3 will never leave a head hurt youth athlete in danger.**

BPE Youth Fast-Track's Honor Code and Brain Wellness Best Practices offers immediate hope for the future brain health and development of youth athletes, while preserving the sports they love to play. As the ominous news on sports head injury escalates, and the size, speed and strength of youth athletes evolves, clinician scientists must exhaustively analyze parallel neuroscience developments on brain-functioning and wellness to create inventive quick-win solutions to offset these ongoing challenges. This *significantly empowers the Big-3 by arming them not only with advanced head injury knowledge, but with tangible brain improvement solutions as well.*

We were strongly encouraged to write this book by our NFL clientele who said it would improve young lives based on their experience with Brain In Play's original BPE-12 system and having recently been youth athletes themselves. We agreed but insisted on creating a fast-track version that addresses the core issues specific to middle/high school and college athletes, while simultaneously engaging parents and coaches in this *disruptive innovation process.* This is because youth players (to date the least involved youth sports head injury group) must always be the priority (*not just in words but action*), and integrated approaches that include parents and youth coaches are vital for successful accelerated change: *those closest to the youth sports head injury action* with the most incentive to drive change must all be involved, ideally together. This translates to youth players who have the most to gain (and lose), worried-sick parents who love their kids yet know the value of youth sports, and top coaches who will do whatever it takes to keep kids safe; again, whether this change involves one player/parent/coach threesome, a team of threesomes, or school, league and organization-wide efforts. And *as much change as possible needs to happen now supporting players and their brains to be safer for sports – to avoid those incidents of second impact syndrome, disabling persistent post concussive syndromes, post concussive chronic depressions/suicides, and catastrophic paralyses - that could have been prevented.*

Hopefully, that Churchill quote used earlier makes a bit more sense now. While it is true we are far from having all the answers to resolve *sports head injuries,* 'the beginning' is over, as we have more than enough evidence-based data to take action on now to improve things on behalf of youth athletes. Coach Herb Brooks was right, *great moments are born from great opportunity,* and what stands before all motivated Big-3 is the chance to lead forward some basic changes that can improve and save young lives today. Not everyone who can, will act on this calling, likely just those born and raised to do such things. Thus, a final call to action goes out to all Big-3 players, parents and coaches (and others) to spread the word about BPE Youth's Brain Wellness Best Practices, and Code of Honor/Behavior. In parting it is all three authors' express hope that the Big-3, led by players, will embrace BPE-Youth Fast-Track and run with it...the best hedge to reduce the risk of, and prevent head injuries, enhance athletic and academic performance, and accelerate and improve healing.

Aligned with Churchill/Coach Brooks, in July 2014 the American Academy of Neurology released a position statement: *all doctors have an ethical obligation to educate and protect athletes from concussion – with those caring for patients needing to have adequate training and experience in the recognition and evaluation of the existence and severity of potential brain injury*. This acknowledges an improvement opportunity also exists for primary care providers. It is exciting to think what the outcome could mean for youth athletes going forward.

Hopefully needless to say, while this book was designed for and dedicated to youth athletes, athletes and individuals of any age can benefit from its fast-track Best-Practices and Honor Code premises. This includes active/veteran military with histories of concussion numbering in the hundreds of thousands (who hold a special place in our hearts, as all 3 authors spent parts of their careers providing care to active/retired military), and post-concussed adults and seniors.

Before closing I am compelled to mention two young individuals who lived generations apart and left this world far too early, Nathan Stiles and Anne Frank. Nathan's story (Chapter 8) reminds us that no one is promised tomorrow, a young man lost at 17 to second impact syndrome whose life still counts for others every day. Anne, a 15-year-old Holocaust victim whose quote launches chapter 18, shows us that even if one's time is short, a committed person can forever influence and change the world in an instant. Nathan and Anne provided much inspiration during this book's long home stretch.

In concluding we want to express our appreciation one final time to everyone who graciously supported us to write this book. We are especially grateful to those sports head injured families that have experienced the loss of, or the serious head injury of a child or sibling, and are celebrating their lives and/or recoveries by contributing knowledge and awareness to others. Your spirits of love and generosity are an example for us all to learn from and emulate.

Appendix

ABOUT BRAIN IN PLAY INTERNATIONAL

BRAIN IN PLAY™

Innovation for Life

SPORTS AND MILITARY CONCUSSION
RISK REDUCTION, HEALING
& CONSEQUENCE AVOIDANCE
www.BrainInPlay.com

Brain In Play International (BIP) is a privately held company founded by clinician-scientists Bill T. White MSN and Katharine B. White MSN, CPHQ that is in the business of evidence-based brain wellness. We provide prevention, treatment, and consult-training services for sports related concussive and accumulated subconcussive brain injuries, and diseases of aging (Alzheimer's/CTE) utilizing BIP's patent-pending brain optimization services/technologies.

BIP's mission is to improve and save lives by providing client access to brain performance enhancement information and treatment services that increase the functioning, preservation and growth of brain cells. Specialties include:
- Sports head injury prevention: Individual and Team Programs
- Post-concussion recovery services: Adolescent-Adult
- Cognitive Behavioral Therapy: Concussive Depression/PTSD
- Concussion prevention-maintenance elite athletes: youth-pros
- Athletic performance enhancement elite athletes: youth-pros
- Dementia prevention and early intervention.

The Whites are majority BIP owners, with physicians from neurology, gastroenterology and radiology as minority owners and investors.

ABOUT THE AUTHORS

Chief author Bill White MSN is a clinician-scientist and President of Brain In Play International, a company providing prevention, treatment, and consult-training services for sports related concussive and accumulated subconcussive brain injuries, and diseases of aging. For 20 years he served as Chief Operating and Chief Patient Care Officer at Brown University Medical School affiliated Bradley Hospital, the nation's first brain/behavioral health hospital exclusively for youth under 21, while he coached 3 youth contact sports, was president of a youth sports league, instructed in medical/nursing schools, and parented 5 high school athletes - one of whom suffered a post concussive syndrome of many years duration. A member of the American Academy of Neurology, Bill, with his business partner wife Katharine originated Brain Performance Enhancement[sm], a patent pending brain wellness and activation science system to prevent and heal sports head injuries and brain diseases of aging based on Nobel Prize research tenets, from which they excerpted Brain Performance Enhancement for Youth Fast-Track[sm]. With advanced clinical degrees and board certifications in brain/behavioral health, Bill and Katharine are especially committed to improving awareness and treatment solutions regarding depression and other comorbid mental health diagnoses caused or exacerbated by sports head injuries.

Second author Alan Ashare MD is an international youth sports-head injury physician safety advocate with three decades of experience in the prevention and safety management of youth sports head injuries. He originated the *Heads Up, Don't Duck* program for USA Hockey in the mid-90s (adapted today by most sports) and in May 2014 released the leading edge book *The Mechanism of Concussion in Sports* as 1st editor. Alan has organized multiple national and international sports head injury conferences over the past twenty years and closer to home chairs the interscholastic high school medical oversight committee across all contact sports and the Massachusetts Medical Society Student Health and Sports Medicine Committee. Dr. Ashare is Chief of Nuclear Medicine at St. Elizabeth Hospital and A/Prof of Medicine at Tufts Medical School. 'Doc' has long served as Team Physician for USA Hockey Junior Teams in World Championship Play. He is President of the Hockey Equipment Certification Council, Director Emeritus of USA Hockey, and Chairman of the USA Hockey Safety and Protective Equipment Committee. He is Chair of the ASTM F08.51 Subcommittee on Medical Aspects and Biomechanics. A father of four high school/college athletes and grandfather to four more youth players, Alan is a former college football player and fencer and Air Force Medical Officer.

Author Katharine B. White is a clinician scientist and CEO/Co-founder of Brain In Play International and Lighthouse Performance Strategies, Inc. with three decades of experience in healthcare, most at the senior executive level. An advanced practice nurse board certified in brain/behavioral health, she is a former hospital Chief Nursing Officer and was Senior Vice President of Quality at the nation's first horizontally integrated home health agency. Katharine is a serial healthcare entrepreneur and gifted public speaker who was a founding member of Coachville®, designed and directed one of the first family behavioral health programs in U.S. homecare and implemented the country's first internal coaching department in a JCAHO accredited home healthcare agency. In 2007 she originated Healthcare Values-Patient Safety First, an integrated healthcare quality management system unveiled nationally at ASHHRA, the American Society of Healthcare Human Resources Association's Annual Meeting at Disney, CA, which was awarded a master learning designation. She is a past medical-nursing school faculty/instructor and private practice psychotherapist who has served on the boards of, consulted with, or presented to multiple national-level organizations. With Co-Author and business partner husband Bill White, she co-developed Brain Performance Enhancement[sm] and BPE Youth Fast Track[sm], neuroepigenetic brain wellness systems to help prevent and heal sports related head injuries and diseases of aging.

R e f e r e n c e s

1. Breedlove, E. et. al., Biomechanical Correlates of Symptomatic and Asymptomatic Neurophysiological Impairment in High School Football. *Journal of Biomechanics*, vol. 45, no. 7, pp. 1265-1272, Apr 2012.

2. McAllister, Thomas et. al., Effect of head impacts on diffusivity measures in a cohort of collegiate contact sport athletes. Neurology, 2013 DOI: 10.1212/01.wnl.0000438220.16190

3. Singh, R. et al., Relationship of Collegiate Football Experience and Concussion With Hippocampal Volume and Cognitive Outcomes. JAMA, 2014; 311 (18): 1883 DOI: 10.1001/jama.2014.3313

4. Baugh, C. et. al., Chronic traumatic encephalopathy: Neurodegeneration following repetitive concussive and subconcussive brain trauma. Brain Imaging and Behavior, 2012; 6(2): 244-254.

5. McCrory, P. et. al., Consensus Statement on Concussion in Sport—the 4th International Conference on Concussion in Sport Held in Zurich, November 2012. Clinical Journal of Sport Medicine: March 2013 - Volume 23 - Issue 2 - p 89–117

6. Giza, C. et al., Pathophysiology of sports-related concussion: an update on basic science and translational research. Sports Health. 2011 Jan;3(1):46-51

7. Ahmadzadeh, H. et al., Viscoelasticity of Tau Proteins Leads to Strain Rate-Dependent Breaking of Microtubules during Axonal Stretch Injury: Predictions from a Mathematical Model. Biophysical Journal, 2014; 106 (5): 1123 DOI: 10.1016/j.bpj.2014.01.024

8. American Academy of Pediatrics. "High school athletes say concussions won't sideline them." ScienceDaily. ScienceDaily, 6 May 2013. <www.sciencedaily.com/releases/2013/05/130506095407.htm>.

9. American Academy of Pediatrics. "Many high school football players not concerned about concussions." ScienceDaily. ScienceDaily, 22 October 2012. <www.sciencedaily.com/releases/2012/10/121022080645.htm>.

10. CDC. 2013b. Data Sources for WISQARS™ Nonfatal. http://www.cdc.gov/ncipc/wisqars/nonfatal/datasources.htm#5.2

11.   McKee, A. et. al., The spectrum of disease in chronic traumatic encephalopathy. Brain, 2012; DOI: 10.1093/brain/aws307

12.   Ling,J et. al., A prospective study of gray matter abnormalities in mild traumatic brain injury. Neurology, November 20, 2013, doi: 10.1212/01.wnl.0000437302.36064.b1 Neurology 10.1212/01.wnl.0000437302.36064.b1

13.   American Academy of Neurology, Sports Concussion Guideline Press Kit: https://www.aan.com/uploadedFiles/Website_Library_Assets/Documents/3Practice_Management /5Patient_Resources/1For_Your_Patient/6_Sports_Concussion_Toolkit/guidelines.pdf

14.   Churchill WS., Speech at Mansion House, London, November 10, 1942. Quoted in: Shapiro FR. The Yale Book of Quotations. New Haven, CT: Yale University Press; 2006.

15.   Institute of Medicine and National Research Council. Sports-Related Concussions in Youth: Improving the Science, Changing the Culture. Washington, DC: The National Academies Press, 2014.

16.   Nowinski, Chris., Head Games: Football's Concussion Crisis; Drummond Publishing Group, 2006.

17.   Master, C. et al., Importance of 'Return-to-Learn' in Pediatric and Adolescent Concussion Pediatric Annals 41:9 | September 2012

18.   Graham, et. al Sports Related Concussions in Youth. The National Academies Press, October 2013

19.   Public Broadcasting System Health Student Reporting Labs: High School football players discuss the pressure to stay in the game http://www.pbs.org/newshour/bb/high-school-football-players-concussions/

20.   Torres, D. et. al. Sports-related concussion Anonymous survey of a collegiate cohort Neurol Clin Pract August 2013 vol. 3 no. 4 279-287 Published online before print July 2013, doi:10.1212/CPJ.0b013e3182a1ba22

21.   Maher, M. et al. Concussions and heading in soccer: A review of the evidence of incidence, mechanisms, biomarkers and neurocognitive outcomes. Brain Injury, 2014; 1 DOI: 10.3109/02699052.2013.865269

22.   Sporting News: http://www.sportingnews.com/nfl/story/2012-11-11/nfl-concussions-hide-symptoms-sporting-news-midseason-players-poll

23.   O'Kane, J. et. al., Concussion Among Female Middle-School Soccer Players. JAMA Pediatrics, 2014; DOI: 10.1001/jamapediatrics.2013.4518

24. Bazarian,J. Persistent, Long-term Cerebral White Matter Changes after Sports-Related Repetitive Head Impacts. *PLoS ONE*, 2014; 9 (4): e94734 DOI: 10.1371/journal.pone.0094734

25. Breedlove,K. et al. Detecting Neurocognitive & Neurophysiological Changes as a Result of Subconcussive Blows in High School Football Athletes, Athletic Training & Sports Health Care, volume 6, no. 3, pages 119-127, May/June 2014.

26. Johnson, B. et. al. Alteration of brain default network in subacute phase of injury in concussed adolescents: resting state fMRI study. Neuroimage, 2012; 59(1) 511-518.

27. Bouix S, et al. Increased Gray Matter Diffusion Anisotropy in Patients with Persistent Post-Concussive Symptoms following Mild Traumatic Brain Injury. PLoS ONE (2013) 8(6): e66205. doi:10.1371/journal.pone.0066205

28. American Academy of Neurology (AAN). "How well do football helmets protect players from concussions?." ScienceDaily. ScienceDaily, 17 February 2014. <www.sciencedaily.com/releases/2014/02/140217200751.htm>

29. Mayer, A. et al. Diffusion Abnormalities in Pediatric Mild Traumatic Brain Injury. The Journal of Neuroscience, 12 December 2012, 32(50):17961-17969; DOI:10.1523/JNEUROSCI.3379-12.2012

30. Ling,J. et al., A prospective study of gray matter abnormalities in mild traumatic brain injury Neurology December 10, 2013 81:2121-2127; published ahead of print November 20, 2013

31. Society for Neuroscience (SfN). "Concussions affect children's brains even after symptoms subside." ScienceDaily. ScienceDaily, 11 December 2012. <www.sciencedaily.com/releases/2012/12/121211193122.htm>.

32. McAllister, T. et al. Effect of head impacts on diffusivity measures in a cohort of collegiate sport athletes. Neurology, 2014, 62 (1), 63-69.

33. Marchi,N. et. al. Consequences of Repeated Blood-Brain Barrier Disruption in Football Players. PLoS ONE, 2013; 8 (3): e56805 DOI: 10.1371/journal.pone.0056805

34. Breedlove, E.L., et al Biomechanical Correlates of Symptomatic and Asymptomatic Neurophysiological Impairment in High School Football., Journal of Biomechanics, vol. 45, no. 7, pp. 1265-1272, Apr 2012

35. American Association of Neurological Surgeons (AANS). "Brain changes can result from participation in one year of contact sports, evidence shows." ScienceDaily. ScienceDaily, 8 April 2014. <www.sciencedaily.com/releases/2014/04/140408154105.htm>.

36. Bazarian,J. el al. Persistent, Long-term Cerebral White Matter Changes after Sports-Related Repetitive Head Impacts. PLoS ONE, 2014; 9 (4): e94734 DOI: 10.1371/journal.pone.0094734

37.   Cantu, R et. al. *Hit Count Threshold White* Paper http://hitcount.org/wp-content/uploads/2014/01/Threshold-White-Paper-012714.pdf

38.   FIFA: www.fifa.com/worldfootball/bigcount

39.   Mahr, M. et al. Concussions and heading in soccer: A review of the evidence of incidence, mechanisms, biomarkers and neurocognitive outcomes. Brain Injury, 2014; 1 DOI: 10.3109/02699052.2013.865269

40.   Guskiewicz, K. et al. Cumulative Effects Associated With Recurrent Concussion in Collegiate Football Players - : The NCAA Concussion Study JAMA. 2003;290(19):2549-2555. doi:10.1001/jama.290.19.2549.

41.   Albert Einstein College of Medicine. "Frequent 'heading' in soccer can lead to brain injury and cognitive impairment." ScienceDaily. ScienceDaily, 29 November 2011. ‹www.sciencedaily.com/releases/2011/11/111129092420.htm›.

42.   Lipton,M. et al. Soccer Heading Is Associated with White Matter Microstructural and Cognitive Abnormalities. Radiology, 2013; DOI: 10.1148/radiol.13130545

43.   Poole, V. et al., Spectroscopic Analysis of Neuro-metabolic Changes in Female Soccer Players 19th Annual Meeting of Organization for Human Brain Mapping, Seattle, WA, June 2013, 3296.

44.   Koerte, I. et al., White Matter Integrity in the Brains of Professional Soccer Players Without a Symptomatic Concussion. JAMA. 308(18):1859-1861. doi:10.1001/jama.2012.13735.

45.   Chen, J. et al., Neural substrates of symptoms of depression following concussion in male athletes with persisting post concussion symptoms *Arch Gen Psychiatry*. 2008;65(10; 81-89.

46.   Chrisman, S. et al., Prevalence of diagnosed depression in adolescents with a history of concussion.. 0 *Journal of Adolescent Health*, January 2014

47.   American Academy of Pediatrics. "*Children with brain injuries nearly twice as likely to suffer from depression.*" ScienceDaily. ScienceDaily, 25 October 2013. ‹*www.sciencedaily.com/releases/2013/10/131025091934.htm* ›.

48.   Ilie, G. et al., Suicidality, Bullying and Other Conduct and Mental Health Correlates of Traumatic Brain Injury in Adolescents. PLoS ONE, 2014; 9 (4): e94936 DOI: 10.1371/journal.pone.0094936

49.   Levy-Gigi, E. et. al., Association among clinical response, hippocampal volume, and FKBP5 gene expression in individuals with post traumatic stress disorder receiving cognitive behavioral therapy. Biological Psychiatry 2013; 74(11): 793-800.

50.   Strain,J. et al. Depressive symptoms and white matter dysfunction in retired NFL players with concussion history Neurology July 2, 2013 81:25-32; published ahead of print May 24, 2013

51. Lui,E. et al. Mild Traumatic Brain Injury: Longitudinal Regional Brain Volume Changes. Radiology, 2013 DOI: 10.1148/radiol.13122542

52. Levy-Gigi,E. et al. Association Among Clinical Response, Hippocampal Volume, and FKBP5 Gene Expression In Individuals With Post Traumatic Stress Disorder Receiving Cognitive Behavioral Therapy. Biological Psychiatry, 2013; 74 (11) 793-800.

53. Rashmi, S. et al. Relationship of Collegiate Football Experience and Concussion With Hippocampal Volume and Cognitive Outcomes. JAMA, 2014; 311 (18): 1883 DOI: 10.1001/jama.2014.3313

54. McKee, A. et. al. The spectrum of disease in chronic traumatic encephalopathy. Brain, 2012; DOI: 10.1093/brain/aws307

55. Stern R. et. al. Long-term Consequences of Repetitive Brain Trauma: Chronic Traumatic Encephalopathy. Phys Med Rehabil Clin N Am, 2011; 3, S460-S467.

56. Thomas, A. et al. The effects of Aerobic exercise on brain structure. Frontiers in Psychology 2012 3(86) Prepublished online doi: 10.3389/fpsyg.201200086

57. Dusek J, et al. Genomic Counter-Stress Changes Induced by the Relaxation Response. PLoS ONE 2008 3(7): e2576. doi:10.1371/journal.pone.0002576

58. Manoj, B. et al. Relaxation Response Induces Temporal Transcriptome Changes in Energy Metabolism, Insulin Secretion and Inflammatory Pathways. PLoS ONE, 2013; 8 (5): e62817 DOI: 10.1371/journal.pone.0062817

59. Hölzel,B. et al. Mindfulness practice leads to increases in regional brain gray matter density. Psychiatry Research: Neuroimaging 191 (2011) 36–43

60. King's College London (2013, May 6). Effects of stress on brain cells offer clues to new antidepressant drugs. http://www.sciencedaily.com/releases/2013/05/130506181446.htm

61. Wrann,C, et al. Exercise Induces Hippocampal BDNF through a PGC-1α/FNDC5 Pathway. Cell Metabolism, 2013, Volume 18, Issue 5, 649-659.

62. Erickson, K., et al. Exercise training increases size of hippocampus and improves memory. Proceedings National Academy Sciences 2011; published ahead of print January 31, 2011, doi:10.1073/pnas.1015950108

63. Chaddock, L. et al. A neuroimaging investigation of the association between aerobic fitness, hippocampal volume, and memory performance in preadolescent children. Brain Res. 2010 Oct 28;1358:172-83. doi: 10.1016/j.brainres.2010.08.049.

194 · W. WHITE MSN, A. ASHARE MD, K. WHITE MSN

64. Martikainen, S. et al. Higher Levels of Physical Activity Are Associated With Lower Hypothalamic-Pituitary-Adrenocortical Axis Reactivity to Psychosocial Stress in Children. Journal of Clinical Endocrinology & Metabolism, 2013; DOI: 10.1210/jc.2012-374

65. Killgore, W. et al. Physical exercise habits correlate with gray matter volume of the hippocampus in healthy adult humans. Sci Rep. 2013 12(3): 3457. Doi: 10.1038/srep03457

66. Barbey, A. et al. Preservation of General Intelligence following Traumatic Brain Injury: Contributions of the Met66 Brain-Derived Neurotrophic Factor. PLoS ONE, 2014; 9 (2): e88733 DOI: 10.1371/journal.pone.0088733

67. Vgontzas, A. et al. Adverse effects of modest sleep restriction on sleepiness, performance, and inflammatory cytokines. J Clin Endocrinol Metab. 2004; 89(5):2119-26 (ISSN: 0021-972X)

68. Anacker, C. et al. Role for the kinase SGK1 in stress, depression, and glucocorticoid effects on hippocampal neurogenesis. PNAS, May 6, 2013 DOI: 10.1073/pnas.1300886110

69. Joo, E. et al Adverse effects of 24 hours of sleep deprivation on cognition and stress hormones. Journal Clinical Neurology, 2012 Jun;8(2):146-150J http://dx.doi.org/10.3988/jcn.2012.8.2.146

70. Giese, M. et al. The interplay of stress and sleep impacts BDNF level PloS One 2013 8(10):e76050. Doi: 10.1371/journal.pone.0076

71. University of Utah. http:learn.genetics.utah.edu./content/epigenetics/

72. Topol, E. The Creative Destruction of Medicine: How the Digital Revolution Will Create Better Healthcare. New York, ,NY: Basic Books (Perseus); 2012.

73. Dwivedi, Y. Brain-derived neurotrophic factor: role in depression & suicide. Neuropsych. Dis. Treat. 2009; 5: 433-449.

74. Ashare, A. et al. The Mechanism of Concussion in Sports. West Conshohocken, PA.: ASTM International; 2014.

75. Perlmutter, David Grain Brain: The Surprising Truth about Wheat, Carbs, and Sugar--Your Brain's Silent Killers Little, Brown and Company NY, NY Sept 17, 2013

76. Van Eyck, A. et al. Sleep-Disordered Breathing And C-Reactive Protein In Obese Children And Adolescents; Pediatric Slee and Sleep Medicine, 2014: A1265, 10.1164/ajrccm conference.2014.189.1_MeetingAbstracts.A1265

77. Schmidt, A., et al. Green tea extract enhances parieto-frontal connectivity during working memory processing. Psychopharmacology (Berl). 2014 Mar 19. [Epub ahead of print]

78. Kempton, M. et al. Dehydration affects brain structure and function in healthy adolescents. Hum Brain Mapp. 2011 Jan;32(1):71-9. doi: 10.1002/hbm.20999.

79. Hermens, D. et al Pathways to alcohol-induced brain impairment in young people: A review. Cortex, 2013; 49 (1): 3 DOI: 10.1016/j.cortex.2012.05.021

80. Anderson, M. et al. Moderate drinking? Alcohol consumption significantly decreases neurogenesis in the adult hippocampus. Neuroscience, 2012; 224: 202 DOI: 10.1016/j.neuroscience.2012.08.018

81. Bala, S. Acute Binge Drinking Increases Serum Endotoxin and Bacterial DNA Levels in Healthy Individuals. PLoS ONE 9(5): e96864. doi:10.1371/journal.pone.0096864 (2014)

82. Gilman, J. et al. Cannabis Use Is Quantitatively Associated with Nucleus Accumbens and Amygdala Abnormalities in Young Adult Recreational Users The Journal of Neuroscience, 16 April 2014, 34(16): 5529-5538; doi: 10.1523/JNEUROSCI.4745-13.2014

83. Volkow, N. et al. Adverse Health Effects of Marijuana Use; published online June 4, 2014 in The New England Journal of Medicine.

84. Chen, J. et al Neural Substrates of Symptoms of Depression Following Concussion in Male Athletes With Persisting Postconcussion Symptoms Arch Gen Psychiatry. 2008;65(1):81-89. doi:10.1001/archgenpsychiatry.2007.8.

85. Khakhalin, A et al. (2014), Excitation and inhibition in recurrent networks mediate collision avoidance in Xenopus tadpoles. European Journal of Neuroscience. doi: 10.1111/ejn.12664

86. Ahmadzadeh, H. et al. Viscoelasticity of Tau Proteins Leads to Strain Rate-Dependent Breaking of Microtubules during Axonal Stretch Injury: Predictions from a Mathematical Model. Biophysical Journal, March 2014; 106(5): 1123 – 1133.

Appendix: Photo Attributions

[1]: Soccer creative commons licensed (BY) flickr photo by K.M. Klemencic: http://flickr.com/photos/klemencic/9279305713

[2]: DTI Scans creative commons licensed (BY) flickr photo by jgmarcelino: http://flickr.com/photos/gkpics/4542550925

[3]: creative commons licensed (BY-SA) flickr photo by NeeDeeAhh!: http://flickr.com/photos/25975281@N05/3364126518

[4]: Figure 5: Biology Class creative commons licensed (BY-SA) flickr photo by dorothy.voorhees: http://flickr.com/photos/dvoorhees/3353412277

[5]: The US Army Football: creative commons licensed (BY) flickr photo by The U.S. Army: http://flickr.com/photos/soldiersmediacenter/8344961725

Cover Images

Field Hockey Cover Image: creative commons licensed (BY) flickr photo by fh.mum1: http://flickr.com/photos/mercyjagsfh/10320500414

Football Cover Image: creative commons licensed (BY) flickr photo by Erik Daniel Drost: http://flickr.com/photos/edrost88/9639460450

Hockey Cover Image: creative commons licensed (BY) flickr photo by K.M. Klemencic: http://flickr.com/photos/klemencic/5273328124

Cyclist Cover Image: creative commons licensed (BY) flickr photo by johnthescone: http://flickr.com/photos/johnthescone/2527829321

Softball Cover Image: creative commons licensed (BY) flickr photo by K.M. Klemencic: http://flickr.com/photos/klemencic/5642372694

Basketball Cover Image creative commons licensed (BY) flickr photo by Beth Rankin: http://flickr.com/photos/bethcanphoto/377216646

The US Army Football: creative commons licensed (BY) flickr photo by The U.S. Army: http://flickr.com/photos/soldiersmediacenter/8344961725